THE PROTOCOL SCHOOL OF WASHINGTON®

TEA & ETIQUETTE

Taking Tea for Business and Pleasure

Dorothea Johnson & Bruce Richardson

Foreword by James Norwood Pratt

Recipes by Shelley Richardson

BENJAMIN PRESS

Original text by Dorothea Johnson
Additional text by Bruce Richardson
British tea history by Jane Pettigrew
Recipes by Shelley Richardson
Photography by Bruce Richardson
Copy editor: Patsi Trollinger
Photo editor: Ben Richardson

Copyright © 2009 Benjamin Press

ISBN 978-0-9793431-6-2

Printed in Canada

Benjamin Press
PO Box 100
Perryville, KY 40468
800.765.2139
www.benjaminpress.com

THE PROTOCOL SCHOOL OF WASHINGTON®

TEA & ETIQUETTE

Taking Tea for Business and Pleasure

The Fairmont Hotel, San Francisco, California

Table of Contents

Foreword

Afternoon tea is one of the fastest-growing trends in America, and it is riding a wave of popularity around the world. There is an attractive, timeless quality about going to tea; and hotels, country inns, museums, and tea rooms are competing to re-create the atmosphere of a bygone era. No matter where it occurs, there is a calming, eternal charm about the whole affair that is irresistible. Tea beckons us to enjoy quality time with friends and loved ones, and especially to rediscover the art of relaxed conversation.

Afternoon tea conjures up feelings of elegance and gentility. It is, after all, synonymous with civility and blessed with the endearing quality of being just a touch highbrow. The customs and courtesies associated with this most civilized ceremony, however, are disquieting to the uninitiated. Fear of committing "tea faux pas" is on the upturn, as tea is now serving not only a social function, but a professional one as well—an alternative to the business lunch or dinner. This has created an unprecedented demand for learning the essentials of tea etiquette as executives meet in hotel lounges to discuss business over a cup of tea.

While there is infinite pleasure in taking tea, it is also cloaked with a system of rules designed, I believe, to civilize and calm our more primitive side. To me, the ritualized exchange of courtesies at a tea gathering illustrates, in microcosm, the central role of etiquette in human life. At tea, as in any other interaction, we are not free to act merely as we please; but we must act with mutual consideration, as befits our interdependence. Sharing tea provides us with a perfect opportunity to express this truth in action. Observing courtesies, a form of sympathetic coordination, allows host and guest to achieve a harmony that transcends their respective roles. This attitude of considerate harmony can extend also to the inanimate utensils we use and to the very tea itself. In this way, the peace and poetry of life that we all seek can be found reflected in a simple cup of tea.

This book includes elements of both social and business tea etiquette, since you may be called upon to be either host or guest as afternoon tea becomes an increasingly-popular way to entertain. The book begins with some of the fascinating history and customs surrounding the tea ceremony to give you an understanding of its importance worldwide.

I am happy to have Bruce Richardson as a contributing writer and publisher for this new tenth anniversary edition. He has updated all the tea sections with the latest information. In addition, he has richly illustrated this book with colorful photographs he has shot in tea rooms, hotels, and tea shops around the world.

Shelley Richardson has contributed some of her favorite recipes to accompany this most pleasant of dining times with friends or business associates. She has greatly influenced America's tea renaissance for two decades with her creative and delicious recipes found in her beautiful tea recipe books. Her touch can be seen in tea rooms across the country.

While I have made every effort not to tell you more than you really want to know, I have also made every effort to provide contemporary information that will give you the heart of grace to enjoy yourself at tea and to interact with kindness and respect to those around you.

Dorothea Johnson

Blackberry Farm, Walland, Tennessee

Introduction

If someone as formidable as Lady Bracknell of Oscar Wilde's *The Importance of Being Earnest* were to invite me to tea, I'd know exactly what to do: Call Dorothea Johnson! Not even the loftiest and most English ceremony of afternoon tea daunts Dorothea. By the time she got through with me, I could not be intimidated by even so imposing a grande dame as Her Ladyship. In fact, I'd be prepared to enjoy her company as well as her tea and myself into the bargain. A leading American "mannerist," Dorothea has been helping men, women, and children learn manners since 1957. She prepares her students to enjoy life to the fullest by making them secure in life's fundamental social graces. It takes a very little bit of extra poise and understanding to produce a vastly different impression on others—and vastly greater pleasure for all.

My dear friends, Bruce and Shelley Richardson, join Dorothea in making this tenth anniversary edition even more complete. Their influence on America's current tea renaissance is evident in the number of their books found on the kitchen shelves of tea rooms across America. They have introduced us to the new American tea cuisine that combines the best of all tea traditions into a glorious celebration. At their tea table, East meets West, South meets North, old meets new, and all who partake come away refreshed and enriched.

It is a particularly blessed event to herald this updated edition on the etiquette of tea, for this is an arena where coaching will prove invaluable. In the aftermath of the Boston Tea Party, Americans were born with a prenatal disinclination for tea. Today, with the encouragement of trendsetters like

Dorothea, Bruce, and Shelley, we are rediscovering what a healthful habit and adjunct to social joy tea can be. But are we sure we know what we're doing?

The drinking of tea, like the making of it, calls for a certain amount of ceremony or ritual. The steps in the ritual of tea-making follow a prescribed order because they MUST. You cannot pour the tea until it has steeped; you cannot steep the tea until you have heated the water; et cetera. In drinking tea, the ceremony to be observed may seem less logical, perhaps, but it is no less necessary. This is because tea is pre-eminently a social beverage, and any social situation calls for manners. In fact, the ceremonies of teatime can raise our manners to the pinnacle of refinement.

We cannot refine what we have not got, however. A teatime ritual of some sort has evolved in every culture and in every time where tea has played a role. While the Japanese tea ceremony or the use of the samovar may be of passing interest, it is the Black Tea Ceremony

as developed in England that we encounter with increasing frequency in our social and business life today. This is the focus of *Tea & Etiquette*, and we will all be just that much more civilized for learning what this book has to teach us.

One reason tea makes us feel good is because of its physical effects. The caffeine it contains banishes fatigue and lifts our spirits without coffee's jolt or letdown, and at the same time its healthful polyphenols act to calm us. Tea is the only substance known that both stimulates and soothes. But the sense of genial well-being tea imparts comes in large measure, I believe, from the tea ceremony itself. It is an exchange of simple courtesies and the sharing of a simple pleasure that induces a pleasant harmony not otherwise obtainable. Just as it is a ceremony that always calls for using beautiful things—silver, porcelain, linens, et cetera—to enhance it, so also it always allows our most beautiful comportment. All this, taken together, is why tea is one of those things that always makes us feel a little more civilized, and all this is what *Tea & Etiquette* teaches.

"Virtue gone to seed" is what Emerson called courtesy, as if to prove great minds can also have blind spots. He might have been corrected—tactfully, one feels sure—by his great contemporary Goethe, who justly observed: "There is no external sign of courtesy without a deep ethical cause." The authors of this book are on the side of Goethe, not Emerson. If the world we inhabit is ever so slightly more thoughtful and more mannerly, and, if we are more at home in it, this is in no small measure thanks to the effects of tea and to teachers like Dorothea Johnson, Bruce Richardson, and Shelley Richardson.

James Norwood Pratt
San Francisco, California

The Fairmont Empress Hotel, Victoria, British Columbia

1

TEA PAST AND PRESENT

The naming of teas is a difficult matter,
It isn't just one of your everyday games –
Some might think you mad as a hatter
Should you tell them each goes by various names.
   —T.S. Elliott (1888-1965)

Tea Past and Present

The Chinese word for tea is "tcha", as shown in this symbol.

Legends abound about the discovery of tea, with the origins of the beverage shrouded in Chinese folklore. One legend credits the Chinese Emperor Shen Nung, who discovered that the boiling of water made it safe to drink. One day, almost five thousand years ago, as the emperor was waiting for his pot to boil, leaves from a nearby bush fell into the hot water. The emperor drank the liquid and found it tasty, refreshing, and relaxing.

We now call that plant *Camellia sinensis*. It can grow up to 20 feet in the wild. The China plant is very hardy and can withstand extremely cold temperature. The tenacious roots reach deep into the earth to search out nutrients and anchor the deciduous bush to the steepest mountain slopes. Only the top new leaves, a couple of inches in length, are plucked for tea-making.

Camellia assamica, discovered in the northeastern Indian state of Assam, is considered a tree and can grow up to 65 feet if not reduced to the plucking level of about four feet. The leaf is larger than its cousin, *Camellia sinensis*.

Black, oolong, green, and white are the four major families of tea that are produced by different methods of processing the leaf from either variety of tea plant. Different regions, climate, soil, and sub-variety of the plant determine the variations in flavor and appearance among teas of the same family.

Keemun from China, Darjeeling from India, and Ceylon Orange Pekoe from Sri Lanka are all black teas, for example, but they look and taste very different. White tea, originally produced in the Fujian Province of China, is now manufactured in tea gardens in India, Sri Lanka, and Kenya. White tea from each country has a different appearance and flavor just as grapes grown in different regions produce different wines.

Today, Kenya and Sri Lanka are the two largest exporters of tea in the world. Other major tea growers are China, India, Japan, Indonesia, and Taiwan. Turkey, Iran, Brazil, Bolivia, Thailand, Russia, Mozambique, Uganda, Malawi, Bangladesh, Tanzania, Zaire, Vietnam, and Argentina also grow tea commercially. South Carolina and Hawaii are the only states in the United States where tea is grown and processed.

The Birth of English Tea

When the western world began to discover Asia's favorite beverage in the seventeenth century, the port of London served as a major gateway. Ships arrived from exotic locales to the east, manned by Dutch and Portuguese merchants who had set up successful trading agreements with China.

The first advertisement for tea appeared in London's weekly paper, *Mercurius Politicus,* in 1658, announcing that the "Excellent, and by all Physitians approved, China Drink, called by the Chineans Tcha," would be offered for sale at the "Sultaness Head, a Cophee-house" not far from London Bridge. But tea was not yet popular. When the directors of the English East India Company required a suitable gift for their king, Charles II, in 1664, they scoured around and made do with a silver casket of oil of cinnamon and some "good thea," which they acquired from officers on Dutch ships.

Catherine of Braganza helped introduce tea to England when she arrived in 1662 to marry King Charles II. Coming from Portugal, one of the first countries to import tea into Europe, Catherine had grown up drinking tea. She brewed up the exotic herb for her new family and friends at court. It wasn't long before the fashionable new trend spread to all wealthy Londoners.

One city merchant, Thomas Garraway, recognized the opportunities that tea offered and wanted to persuade customers to indulge in this new beverage. His 1660 broadsheet, *An Exact Description of the Growth, Quality and Vertues of the Leaf Tea,* was the first detailed document that attempted to encourage new sales. Among its claims: "The drink is declared most wholesome, preserving in perfect health until extreme old age."

Garraway and his fellow tobacconists, coffee merchants, and general traders purchased their bulk teas in warehouses and sales rooms around the city where goods were auctioned 'by the candle.' By this method, a candle was lit, and when an inch had burned away, the auction hammer was brought down. The East India Company held a monopoly on the importation of tea, and on March 2, 1774, at the Half-Moon Tavern in Cheapside, the company put up for sale a total of 2,715 chests of Singlo tea that lay in the company's warehouses near the Thames. Gradually, tea began to appear in general stores and specialty shops set up by traders such as the Twining family.

Customers were mostly aristocrats or wealthy civil servants. They or a senior member of their household staff made periodic trips to the chosen store and purchased perhaps a pound of green, Imperial or Bohea tea. Families who lived outside the capital had to wait until a husband, brother, or butler paid a visit to London and could procure the desired quantity of leaf.

Tea Infuses British Life

Merchants also stocked porcelain tea bowls, saucers, and pots brought in from China or Japan on the same ships that carried chests of tea. Households equipped themselves with items described as "a box of tin to keep his lordship's tea in coole" or "a red earthen teapot, 6 tea dishes and a sugar box." By 1682, the Dowager Duchess of Dorset owned "two tea potts, twelve blew tee dishes, eighteen white tee dishes, tenn wrought tea dishes, two white tee cupps wrought, one tee table," most likely ordered from London or purchased there.

In those early days, the loose leaf tea was sold direct from the chest into a 'screw' of paper that was often tucked in the top of a box or bag of other goods. Customers could choose from a range that would have included different types and grades - black Bohea (a corruption of Wuyi, the name of the mountains in China where the black tea came from), Bohea Dust, Pekoe, Imperial, Congo, Green Hyson, Green Dust, Bloom Green, and Finest Hyson.

Merchants experimented with special blends to suit individual customers and made note of successful recipes so as to know exactly what to mix next time that client called. It was not until 1826 that north London tea proprietor John Horniman developed the idea of packing a measured quantity of tea into a branded packet. When he decided to use foil-lined paper packets for his Horniman brand, other merchants were reluctant to distribute it, fearing a loss of profits from their own loose leaf blends. Branded packets of tea did not catch on until much later in the nineteenth century.

Tea consumption grew steadily through the eighteenth century, with growing imports from new British plantations in Assam, Darjeeling, and Nilgiri, India, and a little later from Ceylon. London steadily grew as the center of international tea trade. Teas arrived from distant ports to be stored, sampled, valued, and auctioned on British soil. Some of it was shipped off again to British merchants overseas and other buyers.

Clipper Ships Fuel Demand for Tea

The growth in tea business coincided with the era of the great clipper ships, which could plow their way through the rough seas from China to London faster than any ships before them. In earlier days, East India sailing ships had taken up to fifteen months to make the journey from China to London. The first of the American clippers, launched in 1845, cut the trip to less than eight months. These beautiful ships were sleek and graceful, stable and capacious, carrying more than one million pounds of tea per voyage. Chinese stevedores could intricately stack the maximum number of chests into the hold. By one account, they loaded a single ship with 8,000 chests of tea and many bales of silk in less than an hour.

By the mid-1800s, tea was being consumed in almost every home in London and across Britain. Prices were lower than ever before, and most everyone could afford a regular supply. Tea became a symbol of temperance and healthful living among those who were troubled by the widespread consumption of alcohol. Temperance taverns appeared, serving no alcohol, and tea parties became a popular way to raise funds for the Temperance Society.

The word *tea,* an Anglicized version of the Chinese *tcha,* made its way into British vocabulary as tea shops and tea rooms opened in

many parts of London. The first public tea rooms actually opened in Scotland in 1875 when Stuart Cranston decided to install a few tables and chairs in his tea retail shop in Glasgow so that customers could be comfortable while trying varied brews. His sister Kate went on to open a famous chain of Willow Tea Rooms with the interiors and exteriors designed by Charles Rennie Mackintosh. One Willow Tea Room remains open in Glasgow today.

In London, the Aerated Bread Company was the first to recognize the commercial opportunities to be had from serving tea and food to a cross section of the public. Their tea rooms attracted office workers, nannies with the children they looked after, city gentlemen, ladies out shopping, and mothers with babies. A pot of tea was cheap, and all sorts of sweet and savory foods were offered.

Soon there were tea rooms all over London, designed with the comfort of female clients in mind, for this was the first time that women could go out alone or with female friends without having a husband, father, or brother to chaperone them.

Tea in the Twentieth Century

The turn of the twentieth century and the death of Queen Victoria brought a lighter, more frivolous note to British life and a growing passion, especially among the wealthy, for dining out and for traveling. Many of London's five-star hotels were built in the first decade of the century and featured a palm court or tea lounge where guests could take tea to the genteel sound of an orchestra or string quartet.

The mood of such rooms was often colonial, with palm trees, exotic plants, and rattan furniture creating a light, elegant ambience. For those with money and leisure time, a day's entertainment was not complete until tea had been taken in the Palm Court at the Waldorf or the Ritz. In 1912, when the tango arrived from Buenos Aires, everyone became intoxicated by the excitement and extreme flirtatiousness of this risqué dance. Ladies suddenly were appearing in public in dance dresses that revealed their ankles, and afternoon tea acquired a colorful new element.

At the Waldorf, dainty teatime food was served with sherry and tea at tables arranged around the edge of the white and gold ballroom. Dancers could sip some tea and take to the floor. For women who arrived without partners, obliging male dancers dressed as gauchos were glad to swirl them to the moody Argentinian tango.

America Rediscovers Tea

The early twentieth century saw a tea revival in America. Alva Vanderbilt opened her glorious Newport, Rhode Island, mansion, Marble House, for tea parties aimed at raising awareness for the suffragette movement. Specially designed teapots in her scullery bore the phrase "Votes for Women." These thoroughly modern women, invigorated by their right to vote, began driving cars and traveling on newly-constructed roads into the countryside outside the major cities of New York, Boston, and Philadelphia. Local housewives took advantage of these hungry travelers by opening tea rooms in small towns across the northeast, often by simply placing a wooden "Tea Room" sign in their home's front window. Soon, tea rooms began appearing across the country as tea room training institutes sprang up to teach these new tea entrepreneurs how to operate their small businesses.

The Modern Tea Revival

Back in Britain, old tea traditions declined in the 1950s, and all things American grabbed people's imaginations. Tea took a back seat as coffee rose to prominence. Britons still drank tea at home (now in convenient tea bags) and special occasions were often celebrated with tea parties, but for thirty years, London offered no venues to entice families out to tea. Around 1982, tea began to make a shy and tentative reappearance in London. The Ritz and the Waldorf introduced tea dances again, attracting widespread media and public attention. People would go out to tea clutching a back copy of a woman's magazine or tourist guide that had written about the tradition in order to see for themselves what all the fuss was about.

By 1990, tea began a steady resurgence in America as tea rooms began to appear in major cities and small towns across the country. The number of tea purveyors grew exponentially, and tea magazines, tea books, and tea wares were stocked in many retail outlets. Hotels, spas, and restaurants turned to high-quality loose leaf teas as American consumers became more tea- and health-conscious.

The focus of the modern tea movement is about the preparation of quality tea and beautiful foods in contrast to the tea bags and chicken salad sandwiches found in tea rooms fifty years ago. The ritual of tea is a counterbalance to fast-paced American society. Tea's calming and healing attributes are just what women—and men—need to help them cope with the stresses found in the new millennium.

Tea has found new respect as a growing number of young tea drinkers flock to the new blends and flavors found in tea. Tea bars, tea shops, and tea lounges are the norm now in major urban areas and college towns. Many are forsaking their grandmother's Earl Grey and English Breakfast for the trendy new tastes and aromas of iced chai or a matcha latte.

Whether it's a formal tea party or a casual tea event, the ancient beverage continues to infuse its magic into thirsty cultures around the world.

Tea service has become a popular addition at many museums including the Museum of Modern Art (MOMA) in New York City (above right), The Huntington Library in Pasadena, and the Victoria and Albert Museum in London. The place for an authentic French tea in New York City is Payard Patisserie and Bistro (left) on Lexington Avenue.

2

TEA TALES
A FEW OF DOROTHEA JOHNSON'S
FAVORITE TEA TIMES

*Tea's proper use is to amuse the idle, and relax the studious,
and dilute the full meals of those who cannot use
exercise, and will not use abstinance.*
—Samuel Johnson (1709-84)

Tea Tales—A Few of Dorothea Johnson's Favorite Tea Times

The aim of taking tea is to share goodwill, which has led me across the years to spend many happy hours over tea with friends and colleagues. Many of these teas have been purely social; others have led to important business contracts or contacts. All have provided time for reflection, quiet conversation, and, of course, excitement—an important element of life.

For seasoned tea drinkers and those new to these pleasantries, I have described a few of my memorable teatimes. These teas were filled with pleasures, as well as perils, all of which make the cup that cheers an energizing ritual.

Newport, Rhode Island

Newport was a glorious place to live during the late 1960s, with formal entertaining *de rigueur* and afternoon tea a daily happening. Each setting was more beautiful and formal than the previous one.

Sunday high tea with the Weilers in their pink Bermuda-style home on Cliff Walk was always a special treat. Rena Weiler was a du Pont and the niece of Charles Schwab, the financier. Admiral Weiler, long retired from the Navy, was her seventh and last husband. Both Weilers were in their late seventies, but their age didn't keep them from being great party givers and goers.

High tea at the Weilers was an abundant, beautifully presented buffet supper, and while tea was served during the social hour and with dessert, it was not as popular as some of the more potent beverages. This, of course, never daunted Rena. At the end of high tea, around eight o'clock, her butler handed each guest tea in a disposable cup as they walked out the door. Rena claimed it was an antidote to those "other beverages" and made driving safer.

One afternoon tea that I particularly remember was the one to which Jackie Onassis' mother, Mrs. Hugh Auchincloss, invited members of the Officers' Wives Club. Hammersmith Farm was a sprawling, twenty-eight-room estate on eighty-three acres, filled with lovely antiques that bespoke understated elegance. The oriental carpets were faded to a warm hue with a few worn spots, all of which added to the beauty and charm of the place. The sofas and chairs were covered in exquisite muted silks.

A stroll along Newport's glorious Cliff Walk allows a glimpse into the backyards of some of America's most glamorous mansions of the Gilded Age. Mrs. Alva Vanderbilt's imported Chinese tea house stands on the grounds of her famed Marble House.

I sat motionless in a chair, my eyes drinking in the surrounding lived-in elegance. Both armrests on my chair were so frayed I was afraid to touch either one and purposely sat with my arms close to my body, as all Southern ladies are taught to do, and held my teacup waist level as I sipped.

Fearing melancholy, I went to refill my teacup and returned to find that "my chair" had been commandeered by a woman who was busily picking at the threads on the left armrest. How dare she touch those wonderfully worn silk threads! I could only imagine the times Jackie had sat in that chair, and who knows the other famous people, including President Kennedy. After about five minutes, the "thread picker" rose from the chair as her left hand found her jacket pocket. At last, I could reclaim "my chair" and continue to savor this room; but as I sat down I saw that a large patch of the fabric had

Prior to Ming Dynasty China, tea was normally consumed from the vessel in which it was prepared. As described by the tea master Lu Yu, this special bowl had to be large enough to accommodate the implements and actions of tea brewing, though compact enough to be held comfortably in the hands for consumption. The term for this versatile piece of equipment was simply chawan *(tea bowl). It was during the Ming dynasty that tea preparation gave rise to a smaller vessel called* gaiwan *(covered teacup).*

been picked and pulled from the left armrest. Horrified that someone would think I had done this terrible thing, I sprang from the chair, distanced myself from it, and remained standing for the duration of "Tea at Hammersmith Farm."

My favorite "Newport Teas" were hosted by Hope Johnston, wife of the admiral who commanded the Navy base. Schooled in Europe, Hope was an elegant, aristocratic woman who knew more about entertaining than anyone I had met. I liked to observe how she did things, because each occasion was a learning experience. Of course, it was enormously helpful to her that she had a first-rate staff at hand.

At one such tea, I had properly gone through the receiving line and executed the obligatory greetings to the other ladies when Hope beckoned to me. I hastened to her side as she commanded, "Dorothea, keep an eye on the finger sandwiches; one of the stewards is ill." Well, I was absolutely flattered and honored to police those finger sandwiches. The tray looked full and beautifully arranged, and I walked a few steps away to get a cup of tea only to return and find the tray practically empty, yet no one had been near this area of the table. Puzzled, I went to the kitchen for replacements, only to have this supply vanish within minutes.

Back to the kitchen I went, but this time I decided to keep my eyes on the filled tray. Very shortly, I spotted a hand emerging from under the skirted table, groping for the sandwich tray. I bent down and carefully lifted the long tablecloth to find the Johnstons' twelve-year-old son, Means III, under the table hosting his own party with Mr. Dog, the schnauzer, as guest of honor. He politely greeted me with, "Oh, hello, Mrs. Johnson. It's very nice to see you."

Republic of China

As the guest of a prominent Chinese business owner, I dined in many restaurants in Taiwan that were not frequented by tourists. One particular restaurant stands out vividly in my memory because my host said, "Anna Chennault always goes there; it is the best." Anna Chennault was the widow of the famous World War II Flying Tigers hero, General Claire Chennault.

Several of the restaurant staff approached our table, bowed, and never turned their backs to us as they served or when they exited the room. A covered cup was placed first in front of me, then the other two Americans, and lastly our host. Fearing the unknown, I hesitated to touch the cup and, timidly whispered to my host, "Please explain."

"Lift the lid and look inside and see the tea," he coaxed. I saw leaves floating in tea and wondered how I could drink without swallowing most of them. He quickly showed us how to use the lid to hold back the leaves as we drank the tea. As one constantly in pursuit of new dining experiences, this was, I thought, a heady venture. The food was the best, just as our host had promised.

Washington, D.C.

I met Mrs. Frederick Chien, wife of the ambassador to the United States from the Republic of China, at a social event. During our conversation, I relayed my covered teacup experiences, which seemed to please her. Within a few days, I received an engraved dinner invitation to Twin Oaks, the ambassador's residence, along with a personal note telling me that tea would be served just as I had enjoyed it in Taiwan.

The reader should be aware that this took place before former President Jimmy Carter extended formal diplomatic recognition to the People's Republic of China on the mainland in 1979. Part of the deal was to "derecognize" the Republic of China on Taiwan in just about every category except trade.

There were several Americans at the dinner, and I persuaded Mrs. Chien to demonstrate how to properly drink from the covered cup. She did, and it was a huge hit! On each visit during the following years we always drank from a covered cup, called the *gaiwan*.

Twenty years later, I met the incredibly urbane James Norwood Pratt, who is recognized as one of America's leading tea experts. Norwood is one of those responsible for this country's newfound knowledge and passion for tea.

I was elated when he agreed to come on board as The Protocol School of Washington's® tea expert. As our tea guru, his first command was, "Get me three dozen gaiwans! I will need them to properly demonstrate their usage."

"Right away, Master Pratt, just tell me where," I replied. Norwood's tea tutorings were always a highlight of our tea trainings. This man has more admirers, including *moi*, than anyone I know.

Tea in the Dining Room

I was invited to a Sunday afternoon tea by the charming wife of a German diplomat. They had rented a lovely old house in Georgetown and filled it with fine European and American antiques.

The dining room table, in this case, was treated as a large tea table; no placecards were set and each guest took a seat at the table, a custom that is followed in many European countries. The tea tray was placed at one end of the table, where the hostess sat; the food, the little plates, and napkins were in the middle.

As we sat enjoying each others' company, the beauty of the room, the tea, and food, the man and woman across the table appeared to be quite angry and exchanged rather heated words. I heard her say, "Well, how dare you!" And he replied, "How dare I what?" Followed by her, "If you do it once more I shall tell my husband." He replied, "How can I do it once more when I have not done it at all?"

I was astounded at such behavior. People simply don't fight at teas. They fight at bars, but not in someone's elegant Georgetown dining room during afternoon tea. Just when the argument reached a fever pitch, just when I expected her to empty her teacup in his face, our host rose, walked around the table, stood between the feuding pair, and said in a most diplomatic way, "Excuse me, please," as he dropped to his knees, lifted the tablecloth and pulled his dog, Fritz (a Weimaraner) from under the table. Fritz had apparently been rubbing his nose against the woman's knees, begging for food no doubt, while she was convinced the man seated next to her was making passes under the table.

We all had a good laugh and begged our hosts to let us borrow dear Fritz to liven up our parties. Alas, Fritz was not available as party entertainment.

McLean, Virginia

A client, the CEO of a high-tech firm, called me and said, "Dorothea, I have been invited to tea by this Brit, and I think I need some help. My wife has said, 'Be sure to hold out your pinkie when you pick up the teacup.'" I gently told him, "Be sure you don't hold out your pinkie. Now with that settled, tell me about the times you have drunk tea."

He answered, "When I was a little boy and had a cold, my grand-mother always gave me tea and honey. What I really need is to drink tea, talk business, and not look like a clod."

We set a date for him to join me at my office for a tea tutorial. He was a very attentive pupil as we practiced the rudiments of taking tea, and he never raised his little finger.

As my tutoring was drawing to an end, I extracted two promises from him. Promise number one: Drink tea each afternoon instead of coffee. After all, he needed the practice. I had demonstrated how to make a pot of tea and even supplied him with a tin of my favorite Darjeeling and a tea filter. Promise number two: Call and debrief me the day after the tea date, which was to take place five days later.

Right on schedule, he called, and his voice told me everything had gone well. "I felt comfortable from start to finish, while the other two Americans appeared quite awkward during the eating part and didn't seem to relax until near the end; I felt cool and confident throughout tea."

American tourists are easily spotted in London because they try hard to keep their pinkies extended while holding their teacups. Tearooms, such as the Conservatory at The Lanesborough Hotel (below), encourage their tea guests to forget about all those old caricatures.

I have had the pleasure and honor of attending tea ceremonies both in Japan and at the Embassy of Japan in Washington, D.C. James Norwood Pratt expressed my reaction perfectly in his marvelous book, *The Tea Lover's Treasury*, when he wrote: "Life is too short to attend enough Japanese tea ceremonies to form an intelligent opinion of them."

While it may be impossible for the casual onlooker to understand what she or he is witnessing, the Japanese Tea Ceremony undeniably gives you something to think about. Practitioners and students not only in Japan but around the world devote lifetimes to *cha-no-yu* ("hot water for tea")—beyond doubt the most ritualized way of taking tea ever practiced. But becoming an expert at performing this ritual is not the point. Students of The Way of Tea eventually realize that the formalities and rules

are not meant as an end in themselves. They are intended to express, through the serving and receiving of a cup of tea, a certain understanding of life itself.

It is, I believe, just as James Norwood Pratt has written: "The Japanese cult of the tea ceremony aims beyond beauty, whether of objects or of comportment, at glimpses of the Ultimate." I am not a student of the Japanese Tea Ceremony, but it has helped me understand that etiquette ultimately depends upon a state of mind. The soul of politeness is not a question of rules but of tranquility, humility, and simplicity. And in the taking of tea, it finds perhaps its most perfect expression.

Osaka, Japan

I was fortunate to have a friend who had lived in Japan for almost two years when I arrived there for a two-month stay. She patiently explained the rituals of the tea ceremony and even performed her modified, albeit Americanized version, all of which I found enormously fascinating.

Within days, an invitation arrived to participate in a tea ceremony. We called upon our hostess three days before the tea to accept and to express our gratitude.

The day of the tea, we gathered with another guest in the waiting room twenty minutes before the time stated on the invitation. The seating order was established then with the honor bestowed on the mother of a German diplomat. This procedure works two ways: The seating order is often predetermined, or it is decided after the guests arrive, beginning with the eldest or highest ranking and ending with someone well-versed in the ceremony. I felt very fortunate: The well-versed someone was my friend.

The first part of the ceremony began when the hostess entered, bowed silently, and we bowed in return. Then the hostess left the room. From this moment forward, everything that happened was rigidly set. We arranged ourselves in the prescribed order and changed into clean socks. Then we left all of our belongings in the waiting room and took the path through the garden to the teahouse, or *sukiya*.

The four best known green teas of Japan are (top to bottom below) sencha, bancha, genmaicha, and matcha, used in the Japanese Tea Ceremony.

Teahouses vary in size, although the ones I saw in Japan were approximately nine feet square. Entrance to the *sukiya* was through a low, small door. The intent is to humble high and low alike. After cleansing our hands in basins, we crawled one at a time through the door to the tea room. Once inside, it was our duty to turn and rearrange our shoes and move them out of the way. Inside the tea room, we went to the *tokonoma,* an alcove containing a scroll, and bowed again. After the last person had entered, we seated ourselves, in the predetermined order, on rice mats called *tatami* and talked quietly among ourselves. We praised the garden, the *tokonoma*, and the fragrance of the incense.

The hostess entered, personally greeted each guest, and then lighted incense in the charcoal. The honored guest then requested, on behalf of the others, that we be permitted to admire the incense case, which is always an heirloom of the family.

A light meal of many small courses followed. One was expected to always say, "O-saki ni," anytime one did anything before another guest. At the end of the meal, we retired to the garden to relax, listen to the wind, and chat quietly among ourselves. During this time, our hostess was busy preparing the tea utensils, tidying the room, and exchanging the scroll for a flower arrangement. A hostess may let her guests know she is ready for them by sounding a gong or appearing and bowing silently. Our hostess chose to bow.

We re-entered the *sukiya* and admired the flower arrangement. Next we looked at the kettle, the fire, and the tea caddy before taking our seats on the *tatami*. Our hostess returned and prepared a thick tea called *koicha matcha*. This thick tea was passed from guest to guest in one big tea bowl. The etiquette of drinking in this manner required that I place the silk cloth on my left palm, then carefully set the bowl on the cloth and steady it with my right hand. Then with a nod and an "O-saki ni" to the next guest, I turned the bowl twice clockwise so that the design was facing away. After taking three-and-a-half sips, I put the bowl down, picked up my little cloth, and wiped the edge of the bowl from which I drank. Then I turned it with the design facing me again and passed it to the guest on my right.

After each guest drank from the bowl, it was returned to the hostess, who passed it back to us to examine. She told us the history of the bowl. Our duty as guests was to inquire about and examine carefully every utensil used in the tea preparation. To remain silent would have been offensive. Then a thin tea called *usucha* was served with small cakes. The overall feeling was far more relaxed than at any other time. Each of us was served tea, one at a time, in separate bowls. The only firm etiquette in drinking this tea was to wipe the edge of the bowl I drank from with my thumb and index finger and then wipe those on my napkin.

The utensils were put away with care and reverence. We expressed our gratitude, and the tea ceremony was over. More than four hours had slipped by since our hostess first bowed to us in the waiting room. It barely seemed like an hour, and we marveled at how totally relaxed and at peace we felt.

The emerald green foam found in a bowl of matcha is the result of whisking the powdered green tea with hot water.

Each of us sent our hostess a thank-you note, which was delivered by messenger, not by mail. An alternative would have been to visit our hostess and offer thanks in person. Both methods were considered quite proper. While this particular tea ceremony is a common one, it is not the only style of tea ceremony offered. However, it is typical of the tea ceremonies I participated in while in Japan. The length of time may vary as witnessed at several tea ceremonies in the Washington, D.C., area. At all of the teas, hosted by women from the Embassy of Japan, the way one conducted oneself was important. We watched each other closely to make sure we were doing the right thing, and we made every effort to appreciate the tranquility and beauty of this most ritualized way of taking tea.

My first encounter with the tea dance occurred in the early 1950s at the Cavalier Beach Club in Virginia Beach, Virginia. During the summer season, there was a dance every day of the week. This was the place to go, see, and be seen. The Beach Club, as it was known, was quite exclusive, with a clientele of members, guests of members, and guests of the Cavalier Hotel.

A doorman opened the closely guarded entrance, and one had to present a membership card to the receptionist, who checked it against her list. Inside the club, one walked down a corridor leading to a huge, open outdoor area overlooking the Atlantic Ocean. Tables and chairs crowded the borders of the dance floor on three outdoor areas while the orchestra occupied the center of the fourth enclosed area, with additional tables and chairs filling the remaining space.

The tea dances began at four o'clock, and the place was jumping by 4:30. These were friendly gatherings, where everyone had a wonderful time dancing to the orchestra and visiting at various tables. Women dressed in their loveliest tea dresses, the men wore suits and ties, and children dressed like young ladies and gentlemen. Girls danced with fathers and grandfathers, while boys danced with mothers and grandmothers. And the boys and girls even danced with each other. Time seemed to fly by until around 6:00, when people started drifting out to go to dinner or perhaps a party at someone's home.

Today, afternoon tea dances and tango teas are becoming very popular again as hotels and country clubs eagerly embrace their return. The arrangements are much the same as for an evening dance. The curtains are drawn, the lights dimmed, and candles lighted.

Decorations may be as simple or elaborate as the establishment or host chooses. When the tea dance is held during a particular holiday — Valentine's Day, for example — the theme would naturally center around the color red with hearts prominently featured.

Tea sandwiches, cakes, tea, and coffee are served. Bowls of fruit punch are placed on a separate table, and a bar serves stronger drinks. Guests go to the table and are served tea or coffee. They help themselves to the sandwiches and cakes, which they eat standing or seated at tables with friends.

The hours may vary, but it's generally accepted that tea dances take place from three to five o'clock or four to six o'clock. The time, of course, may be stretched slightly in either direction.

In the 1920s, tango tea dances at The Waldorf were an essential part of London's social life. Today, modern tea guests may step back in time to an age of elegance with an afternoon of music provided by a five-piece band at the renowned Waldorf Hotel Champagne Afternoon Tea Dance (above). The Floral Hall at London's Royal Opera House (left) puts aside its bar to host twenty tea dances each year for those eager to foxtrot, tango, and quickstep their way around the tea table.

MAZAWATTEE TEA.

"AND TRUE LOVE-KNOTS LURKED IN THE BOTTOM OF EVERY TEA-CUP."
(From a Picture by G. Sheridan Knowles, R.I.)

3

HOSTING AN AFTERNOON TEA AT HOME

...sheltered homes and warm firesides – firesides that were waiting, waiting for the bubbling kettle and the fragrant breath of tea. —Agnes Repplier *To Think of Tea*

ATTEE TEA.

Hosting an Afternoon Tea at Home

No one is quite sure when afternoon tea was introduced into English society, but the ceremony became widespread by the 1840s. Credit is given to Anna, seventh Duchess of Bedford, who, because of the long hours between lunch and the evening meal, suffered from afternoon "sinking spells." She remedied them with a tray of tea, bread and butter, and cake. Unable to give up her delightful new habit, she began sharing it with friends. As the price of tea fell during the reign of Queen Victoria, afternoon tea soon progressed from a simple "drink with jam and bread" into a full-blown social event among the English aristocracy.

History, however, places afternoon tea in France much earlier. Tea arrived in Paris twenty years before it found its way into English homes. Madame de Sévigné (1626-1696) referred to "five o'clock tea" in a letter to a friend and mentioned her surprise that some people take milk in their tea.

The traditional time for afternoon tea is four o'clock. Today, most hotels and tea rooms in America serve from three to five o'clock with the hours often stretched slightly in either direction. Along with a choice of teas, there are three distinct courses: savories (tiny sandwiches) first to blunt the appetite, then scones, and finally, pastries. Afternoon tea has also been called "low tea" because it was taken at low tables placed beside armchairs or couches. Many hotels and tea rooms mistakenly call it "high tea." High tea is an evening meal served with a pot of tea and is usually less elegant than afternoon tea.

An afternoon tea is a delightful and inexpensive way to entertain a small or large group. Success and enjoyment require three elements: an honest feeling of friendliness, the offering of hospitality, and the tradition of honoring the guest.

Dorothea Johnson

To honor

Trudy Jones

Tea

Wednesday, October the fifth

Four o`clock

1401 Chain Bridge Road

McLean, Virginia

Please Respond
821-5613

Invitations

Invitations may be extended and accepted by telephone, face-to-face, or by mailing them at least a week in advance. Depending on the geographic location, perhaps two weeks or longer in advance is not unreasonable. Invitations may be informal or engraved, hand-written in calligraphy, or prepared by a calligraphy computer program.

Invite a close friend or two to serve as "pourers" and set up a schedule of when each will be "on duty" dispensing tea. No one should pour for more than fifteen or twenty minutes. It is an honor to be asked to pour tea. The pourer is considered the guardian of the teapot, which implies sterling social graces and profound trust.

Time

Traditional teatime is four o'clock; however any time between one and five o'clock is appropriate for certain areas.

Guest of Honor

When you extend the invitation, let your guests know whom you are honoring.

Dialogue: "Mary, I am hosting a tea in honor of Trudy Jones, and I would be pleased if you could attend." When there is a guest of honor, it is your duty as host to stand with that person near the entrance of the room and introduce each arriving guest to the guest of honor. When the tea is over, guide your guest of honor back to the room entrance to say good-bye to your guests.

Etiquette used to dictate that no one depart a function until the guest of honor had left the premises. The exception was when the guest of honor was also a house guest. In today's social gatherings, you will find this rule practically nonexistent.

The protocol of the guest of honor departing first, however, is still practiced at diplomatic and official functions. At the White House, the guest of honor departs, and then others are free to leave. This protocol is practiced universally at events where world leaders are in attendance.

Equipment

If it is not a large formal tea, a silver tray and tea service are not necessary. A china tea set, consisting of a teapot, a creamer for the milk, a sugar bowl, an optional pitcher of hot water (for those who prefer weak tea), and a plate for lemon slices arranged on a wooden or glass tray are fine. The tea tray and china tea set are placed at one end of the table. On the right, set out the necessary number of cups and saucers and teaspoons to accommodate your guests. Plates, flatware, and tea napkins are placed on the left. Platters of refreshments may include tea sandwiches in fancy shapes, and various kinds of nut breads, cakes, pastries, and cookies.

When the tea is small, the hostess may pour tea for a short period of time and then ask a friend to take her place. This frees her to spend more time with her guests. Each guest tells the pourer his or her preference, that is tea with milk, sugar, or lemon. The pourer serves the tea, and the guest helps himself or herself to refreshments. If it is a small tea, guests sit down. Otherwise, it is a stand-up affair.

At a large tea party, circulate around the room, talking to your guests and seeing that everyone has met and is comfortably enjoying the party.

Candles

Lighted candles add so much atmosphere to an afternoon tea, but there is a candle etiquette to be observed: Curtains are drawn when candles are lighted.

Teapots

The earliest teapots were wine jars (ewers). The Japanese and Chinese used them to hold the boiling water that was poured onto the leaves in small bowls. The Dutch East Indies Company packed Chinese porcelain teapots and cups into chests of tea to give their ships added ballast. These imported tea wares were copied by English porcelain makers.

Josiah Wedgwood perfected a method for uniformly coloring the earthenware produced by his company. His elegant plates came to the attention of England's royal family, and in 1765 Queen Charlotte commissioned him to make a tea service. The Queen gave her permission to christen his service "Queen's Ware." Before long, every aristocrat in England wanted to own Queen's Ware, just as the French patronized Sèvres and Limoges. As time passed, manufacturers began to create teapots in extravagant designs.

Flatware

Flatware is necessary at teas in the following situations:

• When serving cake that is very soft and sticky or filled with cream, forks must be laid on the tea table.

• If jam or cream is to be eaten on scones or bread, there must be knives or butter spreaders.

• If there are dishes with jam and cream where everyone takes a portion, each dish should have its own serving spoon. Diners should never use their own utensils to dip into the jam or cream dish.

• When seated at a table in a private home or in a tea room, there should be at each place setting a knife or butter spreader on the right side of the plate and a fork on the left side.

• A teaspoon may be placed on the saucer holding the cup or to the right of the knife.

London's Silver Vaults offer one of the world's largest retail markets for antique tea wares. It's a great place to add to your collection of flatware or rare silver teapots like the one above.

The teacups you use today for your tea have handles, but this was not always the style. Chinese tea bowls influenced the first European teacups. These dainty little bowls did not have handles or saucers. At first, the English made teacups without handles in the traditional Chinese style. Not until the mid-1750s was a handle added to the cup to prevent ladies from burning their fingers. This improvement was copied from a posset cup, which was also used for hot beverages. (A posset is a hot drink made of milk with wine, ale, or spirits.)

The saucer was once a small dish for sauce; hence the name. Later it moved to its present position under the cup, which is now regarded as incomplete without it. In late Victorian and Edwardian days, some tea drinkers poured their tea into their saucers to cool before sipping. This is what writers of the period meant by "a dish of tea." Today this would be considered improper, and one would appear cloddish drinking from the saucer.

The practice of drinking tea from the saucer with two hands brought about a small dilemma: Where do you place the teacup? It would be improper to place a teacup onto a wooden table without protection from possible water rings. The English porcelain makers—and later the pressed glass industry—invented cup plates, just the size of the cup bottom, to stand between the cup and the table. These were quite popular, and collectable, until the early twentieth century.

It was also proper in the late seventeenth century for a lady to signal she had sipped enough tea by laying her spoon across the top of her cup, tapping the cup lightly with the spoon, or turning the cup upside down. All of these actions are considered rather outdated today.

Teacups and saucers in the Victorian age, such as the Royal Worcester teacup below, were larger than modern cups and saucers. Hot tea, poured from the cup, could cool in the saucer before drinking.

The Fairmont Lake Louise Hotel, Banff National Park, Alberta

How to Hold Cups and Saucers

Place the saucer holding the cup in the palm of your left hand and move it forward to rest on the four fingers, which are slightly spread apart. Steady the saucer with your thumb resting on the rim. A left-handed person simply reverses the procedure.

A handled cup is held with the index finger through the handle, the thumb just above it to support the grip, and the second finger below the handle for added security. The next two fingers naturally follow the curve of the other fingers. It is an affectation to raise the little finger, even slightly.

The crooked, extended pinkie dates back to the eleventh century Crusades and the courtly etiquette of knighthood. In ancient Rome, a cultured person ate with three fingers and a commoner with five. Thus, the birth of the raised pinkie as a sign of elitism.

This three-fingers etiquette rule is still correct when picking up food with the fingers and handling various pieces of flatware. Etiquette books, however, do not offer instructions on extending a crooked pinkie. This affectation is, no doubt, descended from a misinterpretation of the three-fingers versus five-fingers dictates of dining etiquette in the eleventh century.

Teacup Faux Pas

- Cradling the cup in one's fingers when it has a handle.
- Swirling the liquid around in the cup as if it were wine in a glass.

The Gaiwan

The gaiwan (Chinese covered cup) is held, when not drinking from it, very much like a teacup and saucer are held. Place the saucer holding the cup in the palm of your right hand and move it forward to rest on the four fingers, which are slightly spread apart.

Steady the cup with your thumb resting on the rim. A left-handed person simply reverses the procedure.

To drink from the gaiwan, use the thumb and index finger of your left hand to hold the lid by its knob, and let the other three fingers follow the curve of the gaiwan. Tilt the lid slightly away from your lips so that it serves as a filter holding back the leaves as you drink the liquid. The cup is never removed from the saucer.

Gaiwan Faux Pas

- Striking the lid against the cup.

It is considered poor form in most cultures to make unnecessary noises with the accoutrements one uses while eating or drinking.

A Chinese gaiwan is an exceptional one-step vessel for steeping and drinking white or green teas. Hot water may be added for multiple infusions.

A scene in Bernardo Bertolucci's epic film *The Last Emperor* emphasizes this point with great style. Several Chinese empresses have gathered in a room at the palace and are drinking tea from gaiwans. It is announced that the young emperor will need to wear glasses or eventually go blind. He says decisively: "I will wear glasses!" Of course, it was unheard of for emperors to wear glasses. The dowager empress shows her extreme displeasure at his decision by noisily slamming the lid of her gaiwan onto the cup, an act of rudeness only an empress would dare to commit with such flair.

Handling the Cup and Saucer and Food Plate

When you are invited to tea in a private residence, the guests will be served tea by the host/hostess or a friend who is pouring. After taking your tea from the pourer, it is your duty to serve yourself food from the tea table.

If you are taking food on a small plate, select user-friendly, non-sticky foods that do not require a knife and fork. Find a chair and carefully sit down. Hold the saucer just above the knees and raise the cup to the lips without bending forward. Place the cup and saucer on a side table when you are ready to eat. Hold the plate just above the knees with one hand and eat with the other. When you are ready for a sip of your tea, leave the food plate carefully balanced on your knees, raise the cup and saucer from the table, and sip from the cup as described previously.

If a table is not within your reach, keep the cup and saucer in your hand with the plate balanced on your knees. Remove one or two pieces of food from the plate to the side of the saucer, or eat directly from the plate. You may return for more food, and when you have finished eating, place the used plate on the tray or side table usually reserved for this purpose, never back on the tea table.

A savvy tea host will serve finger foods at a tea buffet that are bite-sized and easy to eat with-out utensils.

Teacup Faux Pas

- Lifting only the cup, leaving the saucer on the table, when you are standing.
- Lifting only the cup when you are seated and there is more than 12 inches between you and the table on which your cup and saucer are placed.
- Placing used accoutrements back on the tea table.

A cup, saucer, plate, flatware, or napkin, once used, must never be placed back on the tea table. The table's primary function is for displaying the foods and the tea to be served. It should look beautiful throughout the tea. Place soiled items on the table or tray that is provided for this purpose.

Stirring a Cup of Tea

One of the most annoying sounds is a spoon hitting the inside of a cup when one is stirring. Stirring a cup of tea is done gently and noiselessly by moving the teaspoon in a small arc back and forth in the center of the cup. Do not allow the teaspoon to touch the sides or rim of the cup. Remove the spoon and place it on the saucer behind the cup, with the handle of the spoon pointing in the same direction as the handle of the cup. Visualize the face of a clock on the saucer and properly place the handle of the cup and the handle of the spoon at four on the clock.

Stirring a cup of tea is done gently and noiselessly by moving the teaspoon in a small arc back and forth in the center of the cup. Do not allow the teaspoon to touch the sides or rim of the cup. Remove the spoon and place it on the saucer behind the cup, with the handle of the spoon pointing in the same direction as the handle of the cup.

Teaspoon Faux Pas

- Leaving a spoon upright in the cup.
- Placing the spoon on the saucer in front of the cup.
- Making unnecessary noise by touching the sides of the cup with the spoon while stirring.
- Letting the spoon drop with a clank onto the saucer.

Tea Spills in Your Saucer

In upscale establishments or someone's home, tea spills may be remedied by requesting a clean saucer. In a very casual setting, it is acceptable to fold a paper napkin and slip it under the cup to soak up the liquid. Remove the unsightly soggy napkin from the saucer and place it on another dish if one is available.

When your saucer has a few droplets of tea, it is acceptable to brush the cup lightly against the saucer rim before lifting it to your lips. Best of all, you can prevent saucer spills by filling the teacup only three-quarters full. This allows room for the addition of milk, if needed. It also provides a bit of room for the tea to swirl when stirred with a spoon.

Napkins

The word napkin derives from the old French *naperon*, meaning little tablecloth. The first napkins were the size of today's bath towels. This size was practical because one ate the multi course meal entirely with the fingers. The ancient Egyptians, Greeks, and Romans used them to cleanse the hands during a meal, which could last many hours. At many such meals, it was proper to provide a fresh napkin with each course to keep diners from offending each other, since it was believed they would get sick watching each other wipe their mouths on filthy napkins. During the sixth century B.C., Roman nobility created what we now call a "doggie bag." Guests attending a banquet were expected to wrap delicacies from the table in clean napkins to take home. It was rude to depart empty-handed.

Today, in all dining situations, the napkin is properly picked up and unfolded on the lap, not above the table level. A large dinner napkin is folded in half with the fold facing the body, while a luncheon or tea napkin may he opened completely. In upscale restaurants, the wait staff are trained to place the napkin on your lap, often with too much of a flourish to suit me. Pause for a moment to make sure you and the wait staff do not reach for the napkin simultaneously.

Napkin Faux Pas: Placing a used napkin back on the table before the meal is over.

Don't wipe your mouth with the napkin. Blot it. Lipstick is never blotted on a cloth napkin; discreetly blot the lipstick onto a tissue before you begin to eat. Don't use a napkin as a handkerchief. The napkin should remain on the lap during tea.

If you need to leave the table temporarily, place your napkin on your chair, not on the table. Push your chair back under the table if the setting is appropriate. In upscale restaurants, the wait staff will refold the napkin and place it on the table to the left side of your plate or on the arm of your chair, a practice I thoroughly abhor, even though they are trained to handle the napkin as little as possible. Return the napkin to your lap when you are seated. The host or hostess picks up his or her napkin to signal the close of the tea. He or she makes certain all of the guests have finished before making this move. At the end of the tea, the napkin is not refolded but picked up by the center and placed loosely to the left of the plate.

Tea Infuser/Filter, Tea Strainer, Mote Spoon, and Caddy Spoon

Tea infusers/filters are used to contain the leaves and permit easy removal of the used tea leaves. Some teapots are fitted with infusion baskets. Tea balls, once a common item found in all kitchens, are seldom used today because they do not allow the tea to expand to its full potential and release the full flavor of the leaves.

Master tea blender John Harney once overheard my complaints about cleaning messy wet tea leaves from the teapot. He handed me a paper tea filter and said, "Try this; you'll never have to clean leaves from a teapot again." John was right. Tea filters work best because they allow tea leaves to expand to their full potential. Plus, they are bio-degradeable and disposable. Few products have encouraged the use of loose leaf tea as have these handy and affordable paper products.

Tea strainers are designed to be held above or to rest on top of the cup to catch leaves that escape from the teapot when the tea is made in the British fashion (loose in the pot). These strainers are commonly found in tea rooms across Great Britain and in American tea rooms where tea is served in the British tradition. When pouring for a guest, simply hold the strainer slightly above the cup and pour the tea. If you are pouring for yourself, the strainer may rest on the rim of the cup. Any errant leaves will be contained in the bowl of the strainer. Return the strainer to its resting bowl in order to catch any tea drips.

A mote spoon or mote skimmer is usually made of silver with holes in the bowl. This device, invented in the 18th century, was used to transfer tea leaves from the caddy to the teapot and also to skim off any stray leaves, or "motes," that may have escaped into the cup. The sharp point on the end was used to unblock the teapot spout if it got clogged with tea leaves. Although seldom used today, it does make an interesting conversation piece.

Caddy spoons have short handles so they will fit in the tea caddy. They were used mainly during the Regency and Victorian periods to convey tea from the tea caddy to the teapot.

Proper Tea Pouring

Tea pouring involves the most stylized and personal element of the afternoon tea ceremony simply because of the intimate interaction between pourer and guest. Tea is always served by the host/hostess or a friend, never by servants. Tea is never poured out, then passed several cups at a time, the way coffee may be, because it cools very quickly. Instead, it is always taken by the guest directly from the hands of the pourer.

Holding the teacup and saucer in his/her hand, the pourer begins by pouring each cup to three-fourths full. Ask each guest the following, "With milk, sugar, or lemon?" Add the requested ingredients and place a spoon on the saucer if it is not already there.

Tea-Pouring Faux Pas

- Filling the cup with tea almost to the rim. This results in messy spills in the saucer, which causes dripping tea as one lifts the cup to one's lips.

Sugar and Lemon Requests

Add the sugar first, otherwise the citric acid of the lemon prevents it from dissolving.

When the Guest Responds, "Plain"

No additions are required. It is not necessary to place a spoon on the saucer.

Milk, Sugar, and Lemon

The habit of putting milk in tea reportedly started in France. The French were enjoying tea long before the beverage found its way to the wealthy homes of London. Madame de Sévigné described how Madame de la Sablière launched the fashion: "Madame de la Sablière took her tea with milk, as she told me the other day, because it was to her taste."

Much of the tea produced in India, Sri Lanka, and Kenya is manufactured to be drunk with the addition of milk. It is a given that milk complements a malty Assam or full-bodied Sri Lankan black tea and that cream masks the taste of any tea. This settled, let's launch right into a hotly debated issue in tea etiquette: Are you a M.I.F. (Milk in first) or are you an M.I.L. (Milk in last) tea drinker?

Milk is poured after the tea. You may have heard or read that milk precedes the tea into the cup but this is not the case. You do not put the milk in before the tea because then you cannot judge the strength of the tea by its color and aroma. A dark Assam tea might taste better with more milk than a lighter Darjeeling tea.

Where did this old milk-first tale come from? Samuel Twining has theorized that milk first prevented early china from cracking in reaction to boiling water. That theory appears rather shaky today since boiling water is not poured directly into the cup.

Good reasons to add milk after the tea is poured into a cup

The butler in the popular 1970s television program *Upstairs, Downstairs* kindly gave the following advice to the household servants who were arguing about the virtues of milk before or after the tea is poured: "Those of us downstairs put the milk in first, while those upstairs put the milk in last."

• Moyra Bremner author of *Enquire Within Upon Modern Etiquette and Successful Behaviour*, says, "Milk, strictly speaking, goes in after the tea."

• According to the English writer Evelyn Waugh, "All nannies and many governesses...put the milk in first."

• And, by the way, Queen Elizabeth II adds the milk last.

Sugar

Sugar cubes are preferable, not only for the ritual of using elegant sugar tongs, but for their neatness. Allow the cube(s) to rest briefly (to dissolve) and then stir gently and noiselessly.

Lemon

Many people enjoy the delicate taste and aroma that a thin slice of lemon adds to teas such as a black Darjeeling or a green Japanese sencha.

The addition of lemon was once reserved for black teas. Some black teas such as a fragrant Earl Grey or smoky lapsang souchong are best enjoyed unadulterated, without lemon or sugar. With the renewed interest in green teas, many tea events now offer both green tea and black teas. There is an added benefit to combining lemon to green tea. Citric acid aids in keeping the healthy green tea catechins viable as they pass through the digestive system. A touch of lemon in your green tea might lead to better health!

Lemon is offered thinly sliced (never in wedges) and placed on a dish near the milk and sugar. A lemon fork (with splayed tines) or a similar serving utensil is provided. The tea pourer or the tea drinker can then put a slice directly into the poured cup of tea. Should you desire another cup of tea, the pourer will remove the slice of lemon from your cup and pour your tea. The tea pourer or you may add a fresh lemon slice. You may also be offered a fresh cup, depending on availability.

Milk and lemon are never used together in tea. The citric acid of the lemon causes the milk to curdle.

Lemon Faux Pas

- Putting the lemon slice in the cup before pouring the tea. Tea is always poured in the cup first.
- Placing a lemon slice on the edge of the saucer in anticipation of adding it to the cup later.
- Transferring the lemon slice from the cup of tea to the saucer. You will end up with your cup resting in a puddle of tea.
- Using the spoon to press the lemon slice after you place it in the cup. The oil of the peel and the fruit's juice will provide the desired essence.

Sketch, London

4

GUEST DUTIES AT A SOCIAL TEA

The most popular nonalchoholic beverage is tea,
now considered almost a neccesity of life.
—Mrs. Beeton (1836-1865)

Guest Duties at a Social Tea

Woody Allen has often said, "Eighty percent of success is showing up." While this may be true in certain situations, it doesn't work for the guests who show up and sit like pitchers waiting to be filled. Good guests sing for their supper, or tea as it may be. The ideal guest's virtues are evident in many subtle ways.

First, remove those gloves as soon as you step inside. One does not shake hands while wearing gloves, even if one is eager to bring them back as a fashion statement. Please, dear tea lovers, let's look on the bright side and hope that we do not see one more woman holding a teacup with gloved hands. It has never been correct to eat or drink with gloved hands.

Gloves have been around for more than 10,000 years, and they evolved from the desire to protect the hands from cold weather and from heavy manual labor. Regardless of the climate, every major civilization eventually fabricated both work and costume gloves. Yet there is nothing to indicate they were ever worn while eating or drinking. One must remember that until the seventeenth century, food was picked up with the fingers and eaten in this fashion or speared with a knife and conveyed to the mouth. Every old etiquette book I have in my library decrees that gloves are removed for eating and drinking. Even the long gloves worn with opulent ball gowns were designed to be unbuttoned and folded back to the wrist area.

Greet your host first but don't monopolize him or her. Mingle with the other guests and introduce yourself to those you don't know. A considerate guest will also introduce those guests who do not know each other. Refer to the next sections of this chapter for social introductions and Chapter Six for business introductions. After getting a cup of tea, help yourself to the food. You may prefer my favorite method and decide just to balance a couple of tiny sandwiches on your saucer and continue mingling. This is a great way to meet others and hone your greeting and conversational skills.

If there are chairs and tables and you wish to sit down, place some food on one of the small plates provided and sit down and chat with the other guests. You may return for tea and food as often as you wish. When you have finished drinking and eating, place the cup and saucer and plate on a side table, never back on the tea table. After an hour or so of mingling with the guests, thank the host and say good-bye to him or her and to the guest of honor. Write a thank-you note within twenty-four hours.

Faux Pas

- Wearing gloves while shaking hands, eating, or drinking.
- Monopolizing the host or guest of honor.
- Failing to mingle with the other guests.
- Heaping too much food on the plate.
- Placing the used cup and saucer or any debris on the tea table.
- Failing to write a thank-you note.

Introducing Yourself

Introducing yourself is how you make yourself known to others. Whether in a social or business context, each time you introduce yourself, you are sharing who you are. It is your duty to introduce yourself at any function, large or small, if no one introduces you. You will never make new acquaintances or expand your horizons by holding back or talking only to people you already know. A good introduction includes your first and last name.

A good introduction includes your first and last name.

59

The Berkeley Hotel, London

Social Introductions

In both formal and informal introductions, the first name spoken is that of the older or more distinguished person. The second name spoken is that of the person being introduced (or presented) to the older or more distinguished person.

Men are introduced to women with these exceptions: According to international diplomatic protocol, women are introduced (or presented) to ambassadors, ministers in charge of legations, chiefs of state, royalty, and dignitaries of the church.

Example: "Mr. Ambassador, may I introduce (or present) Mrs. Hill. She is CEO of Sky Corporation. His Excellency is the ambassador of Germany."

Formal Introductions

Introduce a man to a woman.
Example: "Ms. Doe, may I introduce Mr. Jones. His wife is chairing tonight's event. Ms. Doe's company donated the flowers."

Introduce a younger person to an older person.
In this case, you are presenting a child to an adult.
Example: "Mr. Smith, I would like to introduce Mary Johnson, my daughter."

Informal Introductions
To introduce two persons in a group where everyone is on a first-name basis.
Example: "Mary Smith, I want to introduce Tom Jones."

Introduction involving first names
If you are acquainted with only one of the two persons by his or her first name, then introduce both as Ms., Mrs., or Mr. to be consistent.
Example: "Ms. Smith, I want to introduce Mr. Jones."

Tip: Always add some information that will launch others easily into conversation.

In both formal and informal introductions, the first name spoken is that of the older or more distinguished person.

Example: "Debbie Smith, I want to introduce Mary Hill. Mary and I were classmates in college, and she is here on business. Debbie and I are working on the museum fund-raiser."

Introducing a Number of People

A package of fine loose tea always makes a perfect hostess gift.

Say the new person's name and then give the names of the others in the group. If you cannot remember all of their names, it is correct, acceptable, and practical to say the new person's name and suggest that the others introduce themselves.

Don't use expressions such as "shake hands with" or "make the acquaintance of." Don't tack on "my friend" to one of the names when introducing two persons. It implies that the other person is not a friend.

If you are introducing new arrivals at a party, a round-the-room-tour is not necessary. Introduce the newcomers to the closest group of people and check from time to time to make sure they are circulating.

Family Introductions

Introducing one's spouse:

Never refer to your own husband or wife as Mr. Smith or Mrs. Smith in social introductions. If your last name is known to everyone, all you need say is, "Tom, my husband," or "Mary, my wife."

A man should never say, "Meet the *missus*" or "Meet the *wife*."

If a woman has become well known by a professional name, she should mention her husband's last name when introducing him.

Example: "Mr. Jones, I want to introduce Tom Williams, my husband."

This avoids the awkwardness of the husband being called by the wife's last name.

Clarify their relationship to you.

Examples: "Clay Brown, I want to introduce Grant Robertson, my brother."
"Mary Smith, I want to introduce Ellen Colby, my sister-in-law."

If one's mother has remarried, "Mary Cameron, my mother" or "Harry Cameron, my stepfather."

The Ritz, London

5

GOING OUT TO TEA

The mere clink of cups and saucers turns
the mind to happy repose.
—George Gissing (1857-1903)

Going Out to Tea

As pleasant as it is to host a tea at home, going out to tea is one of life's most delightful pastimes. A hotel lounge or tea room may use various titles to describe its tea offerings. Menus offer *Afternoon Tea, Cream Tea, Light Tea, Full Tea,* and *Royal Tea.* You will also encounter an afternoon offering of *High Tea* in certain tea establishments and hotels throughout America. However, in most instances, they mean *Afternoon Tea.*

Service Defined

Service describes the manner of presenting various dishes. Table service also takes into account the ensemble of objects that are used at the table: linens, plates, glasses, and flat-

ware. The utensils required to serve a special part of the meal are called 'services'—tea service, coffee service, dessert service, fruit service, and so forth. The French call the personnel of the restaurant who are responsible for serving meals the "service."

Cream Tea

This light repast may have originated in the southwestern region of England around Devon and Cornwall. The simple menu consists solely of scones, strawberry preserves, clotted cream, and choice of tea. The clotted cream in this region contains a very high butterfat content. American cream teas may substitute a lighter faux Devonshire Cream, whipped cream, lemon or lime curds.

Light Tea

A lighter version of afternoon tea. The menu includes scones, sweets, and choice of tea.

Afternoon or Full Tea

A complete four-course menu includes finger sandwiches, scones, sweets, cake, and a choice of tea. The addition of finger sandwiches or savories as a first course gives this tea the title of 'full tea.'

Royal Tea

This regal meal offers a choice of tea and a four-course menu of finger sandwiches, scones, sweets, cake, and a glass of champagne or sherry. The addition of a glass of champagne or sherry gives this tea the distinction of being called 'royal tea.'

High Tea

The term 'high tea' is often misused by those who like to gild afternoon tea to make it seem exclusive and refined. Consequently, both consumers and dispensers of tea often mistakenly tack the word 'high' onto what should be simply called 'tea' or 'afternoon tea.' Although often confused with afternoon tea, high tea is not a dainty affair; neither is it synonymous with highbrow. The distinction is important if you wish to convey a certain degree of sophistication. Also, high tea is not finger sandwiches, scones, and sweets. That, of course, is simply 'tea' or 'afternoon tea.'

High tea is a hearty, simple, sit-down meal that originated during the Industrial Revolution of the nineteenth century.

Umstead Resort & Spa, Cary, North Carolina

High tea, in the British tradition, was the main meal of the day for workers who returned home very hungry after a long, hard day in the fields, shops, factories, and mines.

Everything is placed on the high dining table, family style, and dishes are passed from person to person. The menu offers hot or cold hearty and traditional foods such as meat pies, Welsh rarebit, sausage, cold meats, breads, cheese, jam, butter, relishes, desserts, fruits, and tea. High tea was also called "meat tea," because meat was usually served.

One may offer 'high tea' in the form of a buffet supper, and alcohol may also be served.

Tea in a Hotel Lounge

Should you choose to have tea at Browns (below) in London, The Drake Hotel in Chicago, or the Ritz-Carlton Battery Park in New York City, you will often be seated on a

sofa or an overstuffed chair. A low table in front of the sofa will hold the tea foods, cups and saucers, and pot(s) of tea. You may eat in the same manner as you would at a regular table. Should you sit back in your seat and there is an uncomfortable distance between you and your teacup, be sure to lift both the cup and saucer from the table as previously described.

Lobby teas are sometimes called low teas. The term 'low tea' may come from the fact that hotels have traditionally used low tables in their lobbies to hold the foods and tea service presented at afternoon teas.

6

BUSINESS TEA ETIQUETTE

It isn't the menu that matters;
it's the men you sit next to.
—Mae West (1893-1980)

Business Tea Etiquette

Afternoon tea is not just a social function but a professional one as well. In their search for a quiet place to wheel and deal, executives are leading a briefcase invasion of the genteel sanctuaries once the domains of white-gloved ladies. Men and women are learning to say to clients and business associates, "Let's discuss this over tea."

There is, after all, a relaxing, albeit powerful, quality to closing deals over a cup of tea, watercress sandwiches, and scones slathered with strawberry jam and clotted cream. While teatime does involve food and drink, it is the opposite of the business lunch or dinner, both of which can be expensive, complicated, caloric, and intoxicating.

Extending the Invitation

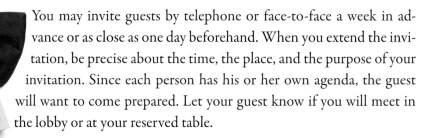

You may invite guests by telephone or face-to-face a week in advance or as close as one day beforehand. When you extend the invitation, be precise about the time, the place, and the purpose of your invitation. Since each person has his or her own agenda, the guest will want to come prepared. Let your guest know if you will meet in the lobby or at your reserved table.

The Host or Hostess

It is the duty of a host or hostess to handle the smallest detail, from the reservation to the tip, the tea, and any items left with the coat-room attendant. Additional duties include leading the conversation. Maintain complete control when you are hosting. There should never be any doubt by the staff at your selected site that you are the host.

Pre-Tea Strategy

• Know the hotel lounge or tea room you are using. Before the day of your business tea, visit the site if it is new to you. Introduce yourself to the maître d' (or captain).
• Pick your table. Select the table at which you wish to be seated and which gives you maximum privacy when you expect to discuss business. Decide where your guest(s) will sit and where you plan to sit.
• Alert the maître d' or captain to your preferred seating arrangement by saying, "My guest will sit there and I will sit here; please pull out the chair for my guest first."
• Always avoid: a table facing a mirror, a table next to the kitchen, and a table near the restrooms.

The Day of Your Tea

The morning of your tea meeting, reconfirm the time and place with your guest or his or her secretary. Since reservations get mixed up, reconfirm with the hotel lounge or tea room you are using as well.

Change of Plans

If you or your guest must reschedule your meeting, call the hotel lounge or tea room and cancel your reservation. Failure to do so makes you appear unprofessional and inconsiderate. Honor a tea reservation just as you would a business appointment.

Arrive Early

Plan to arrive at least fifteen minutes early to check the table and arrange payment of the check with the maître d' or captain. You may sign the check beforehand or ask the captain to hold it for you at his or her station. Excuse yourself from the table as teatime is drawing to a close and take care of the check. Should your guest express concern about the check not being presented, you can simply smile and say, "It has been taken care of." This is a polished method that anyone can use effectively at any place and for any function. An added bonus is the fact that it efficiently solves the problem of a male guest insisting on

The Ritz-Carlton Battery Park, New York City

picking up the check when the host is female. By depersonalizing the event, it is no longer a gender issue. After all, business protocol dictates that the person who does the inviting pays, regardless of gender.

Lobby Meeting

Greet your guest with a handshake and usher him or her ahead of you as you are led to your table. Always offer your guest the preferred seat. It should be the one first pulled from the table, facing out into the room.

When there are only two of you at tea, don't sit across from each other at a square or round table; it is too confrontational. Seat your guest to your right.

When hosting two guests, and the table accommodates four, don't place one guest on each side of you. To do so means you will be moving your head back and forth as if you were at a tennis match. Place the senior person on your right and the junior person across from you, leaving the place on your left empty.

If there are others in your party, indicate where you would like them to sit, and see that everyone is seated before you sit down.

Faux Pas

- Saying to your guest, "Just sit anyplace."
- Involving your guest in paying the check.

Table Meeting

Inform the maître d' or captain that your guest, Mr. Doe, will be joining you at your table. Upon arrival, he will be shown to your table. This is an easy way to recognize a guest you've never seen before. Regardless of gender, the host stands when the guest(s) approach(es) the table and remains standing until everyone at the table is seated.

The Social Side of a Business Tea

The business tea is gaining popularity, and professionals at all levels need to be aware of the social nuances involved. There is always a slight social overtone to tea even though business is being discussed. A professional woman should never assume that a male colleague will pull out her chair; but if he does, she accepts graciously with a "thank you."

Taking Your Seat at a Table

Both women and men use the same method to take a seat. Move to the right of your chair and enter from your left side. Your left hip touches the chair first. (Exception: When the chair is pulled out and space doesn't permit entering from the right side. Be alert to the situation.) Exit the chair from the same side you entered. Always push the chair back under the table after you rise.

A Man Helping a Woman to Be Seated

Thank your host through a handwritten thank-you note on a correspondence card. Mail it within twenty-four hours.

Stand directly behind the chair, with both hands grasping the chair back. Gently pull out the chair. When the woman is half-seated, carefully push the chair in under her. Don't push it in too far. Once settled in, she can adjust it. Release the back of the chair and seat yourself to her left. (If the woman on your left has no one to seat her, you will also seat her.)

A Woman Being Helped with Her Chair

Move to the right of your chair and enter from your left side. Once the chair has been pulled out and you are half-seated, grasp the sides of the seat and lean your body forward while the chair is being pushed in. If you arrive at the table before anyone else, just seat yourself. A nearby wait staff will likely offer to pull out your chair.

When the Tea Is Over

Man: Push back your chair, rise, and reposition it at the table. Then stand behind the chair

76

of the woman on your right, pull back her chair, and reposition it after she rises and moves away from the immediate area. You should also help the woman on your left, if necessary.

The Guest

Be an appreciative guest and participate in the conversation in a professional manner. Concentrate on your host's agenda. Thank your host through a handwritten thank-you note on a correspondence card. Mail it within twenty-four hours. This action will garner you the title "World-Class Executive."

Tip: Every executive should have a supply of correspondence cards. Visit your local stationery store and view their selection. The cards measure 4¼" x 6⅜".

Making a Professional Entrance

Almost everyone watches the entrance to a room. Use it to your advantage when you go to tea. Avoid rushing into the room even if you are a little late. Maintain good posture at all times because it instantly creates an impression of confidence.

To make a strong entrance, walk into the room and pause briefly to spot key persons and to allow others to see you. Don't stand in the doorway, but walk a few feet into the room so you don't block the entrance.

Handshaking—The Ultimate Greeting

We take note of persons nonverbally by their touch, and the way we touch someone socially and in business is most often with our handshake. Shaking hands easily and often creates a favorable impression and influences others to shake hands. The handshake is important because it is the accepted business greeting in almost all countries.

In America's business arena, it doesn't matter who offers a hand first. The person who extends a hand first has a distinct advantage. He or she is being direct, taking the initiative, and establishing control. These are all cutting-edge pluses in the business arena.

In European countries the woman offers her hand first. When a North American businesswoman fails to extend her hand to a European male executive, she loses credibility.

Always Shake Hands

- When introduced to a person and when you say good-bye.
- When someone comes into your office to see you.
- When you meet someone outside your office or home.
- When you enter a room, are greeted by those you know, and are introduced to those you don't know.
- When you leave a gathering attended by business associates.
- When you are congratulating someone who has won an award or given a speech.
- With those nearest you, your host and hostess, and with whomever you meet.
- When you are consoling someone.

Business Introductions

In business introductions, who is introduced to whom is determined by precedence. The person who holds the highest position in an organization takes precedence over others who work there. Gender does not affect the order of introductions. Women and men should be treated according to business protocol, not chivalry.

Introduce Yourself

Introduce yourself by extending your hand; smile and say, "I'm John Doe." Always use both names and never give yourself an honorific such as "I'm Mr. Doe."

Formulas for Introductions

Persons of lesser authority are introduced to persons of greater authority, regardless of gender.

Example: "Mr./Ms. Greater Authority, I would like to introduce Mr./Ms. Lesser Authority."

Protocol: The name of the person of greater authority is always spoken first. The name of the person of lesser authority is always spoken last.

Tip: Don't reverse the order.

Explanation: If you introduce Greater to Lesser, you reverse the order.

Incorrect: "Mr./Ms. Greater Authority, I would like to introduce you to Mr./Ms. Lesser Authority."

A junior executive is introduced to a senior executive.

Example: "Mr. Senior Executive, I would like to introduce Ms. Junior Executive, from the accounting department. Mr. Senior Executive is our director of public relations."

Protocol: The name of the senior executive is always spoken first. The name of the junior executive is always spoken last.

Tip: Don't reverse the order.

A fellow executive is introduced to a client.

Example: "Mary Hopkins, I would like to introduce Jim Smith, my department manager. Jim, Mary is our good customer from Chicago, and she is doing a brisk business with our new interactive software."

Protocol: Clients are considered more important than anyone in your organization, even if your department manager is a vice president and your client is a junior executive.

Tip: Don't reverse the order.

A nonofficial person is introduced to an official person.

Example: "Senator Warner, may I introduce Ms. Doe, president of Doe Exports. Ms. Doe's firm is one of our state's leading exporters."

Protocol: The name of the official is always spoken first. The name of the nonofficial is always spoken last.

Tip: Don't reverse the order.

Introduction Savvy

While making the introduction, refrain from making unnecessary gestures such as touching the people you are introducing or gesturing toward them when you say their names. The less you rely on gestures, the more confident and authoritative you will appear.

Look at each person as you say his or her name. This focuses attention on the individual and makes him or her feel important while you look in control.

Handling Purses, Briefcases, Eyeglasses, and Cell Phones

Simply stated, don't place any of these items on the table at which you are taking tea. Only the tea accoutrements belong on the table.

Purses and Briefcases

Small purses go on your lap under the napkin. Large purses and briefcases are placed by your chair out of the path of the other guests and the wait staff. In a public tea room or hotel lounge, the safest place for a large purse or briefcase is between your feet.

Eyeglasses and Eyeglass Cases

An eyeglass case belongs in your purse, pocket, or briefcase. Should you feel the need to remove your glasses, place them in your jacket pocket or on your lap—never on the table.

Cell Phones

Cell phones should be placed in the off or vibrate mode while at tea. Your full attention should be given to your guests—especially in a business setting.

The Do's of Tea Etiquette— Business and Social

- Do rise, regardless of gender, to greet and shake hands with your guests.
- Do try a little of each course served at tea.
- Do avoid talking with your mouth full. Take small bites, and you will find it is easier to answer questions or join in table talk.
- Do wait until you have swallowed the food in your mouth before you take a sip of tea.
- Do place your napkin on your chair when you briefly leave the table.
- Do place your knife and fork in the 10:20 "I am finished" position when you have finished eating. (For the 10:20 position, imagine a clock face on your plate: tips of knife and fork at ten, handles at four; knife edge turned in, fork tines turned down.)
- Do carry food to your mouth with an inward, not an outward, curve of the fork.
- Do look into, not over, the cup of tea when drinking.
- Do spread the scone with jam first and then cream.

The Do Not's of Tea Etiquette— Business and Social

- Don't place items on the table. This protocol extends to keys, hats, gloves, eyeglasses, cell phones, and anything else that is not part of the meal.
- Don't overload the fork when eating the foods served at tea.
- Don't chew with your mouth open.
- Don't smack your lips.
- Don't reach across the table or across another person to get something. If it is out of reach, ask the closest person to pass it to you.
- Don't touch your face or head during teatime.
- Don't tip up the cup too much when drinking tea, but keep it at a slight angle.
- Don't extend a pinkie when holding a cup.
- Don't try to remove food from your teeth in the presence of others.
- Don't push your plate away from you at the end of the tea.
- Don't gesture with a knife, fork, or spoon in your hand.
- Don't talk about your personal food likes and dislikes during tea.
- Don't place your napkin on the table until you are ready to leave.
- Don't involve your guest(s) in paying the bill.

A smart host will always take care of the bill before or after the event, without involving the guests.

7

FINESSING THE FOOD AT TEA

*A Proper Tea is much nicer than a Very Nearly Tea,
which is one you forget about afterwards.*
—A.A. Milne, *Winnie the Pooh*

Finessing the Food at Tea

Tea food is served either in separate courses or on a tiered stand. Most modern hosts prefer the tiered stand, which allows guests to admire the beautiful selections and the creativity of the chef. We always taste first with our eyes! There is a preferred sequence when plating tea foods on a tiered tray. Begin eating from the bottom tier and work your way up. The positions are as follows:

First tier (bottom): tea sandwiches, which are referred to as savories.
Second tier (middle): scones, pound cake.
Third tier (top): pastries, tarts, or any dessert-type sweet.

Tea Sandwiches (Savories)

The notorious eighteenth-century gambler John Montagu, fourth Earl of Sandwich, is credited with inventing the sandwich. In 1762, when Montagu was forty-four years old, his passion for gambling kept him at the gaming tables for twenty-four straight hours. To keep gambling, he ordered sliced meats and cheeses served to him between pieces of bread. This method enabled him to eat with one hand and gamble with the other.

Tea sandwiches are called savories, tasty tidbits eaten first to blunt the appetite. English tea sandwich selections have stayed the same for nearly a century — cucumber, egg and cress, smoked salmon, and chicken salad. That standard is changing worldwide as travel increases and cuisines blend together. Today's choices include either open-faced or closed sandwiches, wraps, pinwheels, or puff pastries filled with delightful regional delicacies.

Scones

Scones are simple biscuits, often made with currants. I will describe several methods of eating scones, all of them correct, but some hands-on preparation on the part of diners is required.

Using the knife, slice through the scone horizontally, resting it flat on your plate. Spoon small dollops (just enough for a single scone) of jam and cream onto your plate. Never spoon directly onto the scone. Take only the amount of topping needed to eat that one scone and spread one bite at a time, not over the whole scone. Use your knife to dab the edge of the scone with jam, then cream; eat that portion and return the rest to your plate. Sip a little tea, make brilliant conversation, spread new jam and cream, and take another bite, and so on. Between bites, rest the knife on the upper right side of your plate, with the cutting side of the blade facing in. When you have finished, place the knife in the "I am finished" position. (Visualize the face of a clock on your plate. Place the knife in the 10:20 position. The tip of the knife is at ten and the handle is at four. The knife is on the outside with the blade facing in toward the fork, which has its tines facing down.)

Slice through the scone, on your plate; lift off the top piece. Using the knife, spread only the bottom half first with jam and then cream. Place the knife on the upper right side of your plate. You may pick this half of the scone up with your hand, but be ready to use your napkin for those tell-tale signs of cream and jam around the mouth area. This is not a pretty sight! When you have finished, place the knife in the "I am finished" position described above.

Break off a bite-size piece with your fingers. Use your knife to spread on jam, then cream, and convey to the mouth with your fingers. Between bites, place the knife on the upper right side of your plate, with the cutting side of the blade facing in. Repeat the procedure with bite-size pieces. When you have finished, place the knife in the "I am finished" position.

If you don't wish to eat the scone with your fingers, try one of the following styles:
American style: Slice through the scone and lift off the top piece and spread only this half, first with jam and then cream. Secure the scone with the fork in your left hand. With your right hand,

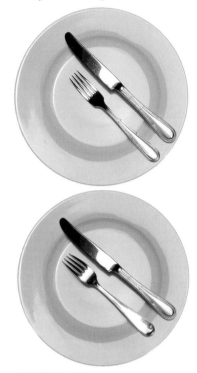

use the knife to cut a bite-size piece. Place the knife on the upper right side of your plate and switch the fork to the right hand. Lift the bite with your fork and convey it to your mouth.

When you have finished, place the knife and fork in the "I am finished" position. (Visualize the face of a clock on your plate. Place both the knife and fork in the 10:20 position with the tines of the fork up. The tip of the knife and fork are at the ten and the handles are at the four. The knife is on the outside, and the cutting side of the blade faces the fork, which is on the inside.)

Continental style: Slice through the scone and lift off the top piece. Spread only this half, first with jam and then cream. Secure the scone with the fork in your left hand. With the knife in your right hand, cut a bite-size piece and convey it to your mouth with the fork in the left hand, tines down. The knife remains in the right hand. Cut only one bite at a time. Should you wish to rest and sip tea, the fork and knife are crossed on the plate with the fork over the knife with the tines pointed down. Picture an inverted V.

When you have finished, place the knife and fork in the 10:20 position with the tines of the fork down.

Finish Position: American Style with fork tines down.

Scones are not always served with clotted cream. Depending on the custom, they are often offered with butter and jam or honey. Spread the butter first and the jam or honey last.

Faux Pas

Putting the scone halves back together, like a sandwich, after spreading on the jam and cream. Or, pouring whipped cream over an unopened scone — like gravy on a biscuit.

Cream

The cream may be called clotted cream, Devon cream, Devonshire cream, or whipped cream. The first three names describe the same super-rich cream imported from Devon, England. If you are served whipped cream, it should be freshly whipped. Use just a dollop on top of the jam as you prepare the scone before eating.

You may use your fingers unless the pastries or tarts are overfilled with cream or otherwise unwieldy. For the latter, secure the pastry or tart with the fork and use the knife to cut one bite-size piece at a time. Convey each bite to your mouth with the fork. You may eat the pastries and tarts in either the American or Continental style.

Iced Tea

What could be more refreshing on a hot summer day than an icy cold glass of tea? Nearly every grand southern home had an icehouse in the eighteenth and nineteenth centuries. Winter ice was cut from streams and placed in subterranean brick or limestone cellars insulated with fresh straw. The first icebox patent was issued in 1830 and cold tea became even more well known. Cold tea recipes began appearing in community cookbooks such as *The Kentucky Housewife* (1839) and *Housekeeping in Old Virginia (1879)*.

One of the most reported iced tea stories came from the 1904 St. Louis World's Fair when Richard Blechynden, a tea vendor, became weary of selling his cups of hot tea in the summer heat. In an attempt to boost sales, he served tea in glasses packed with plenty of ice. This cool refreshing beverage was a hit with fair-goers who then popularized iced tea throughout the United States. Call it *iced* tea, not *ice* tea. Tea with ice in it is an "iced" beverage.

A Glass of Iced Tea

Iced tea should be served in a tall glass that is placed on a saucer or a small plate such as a bread and butter plate. The long iced teaspoon is placed on the outer right of the flatware. You may even place it at a slight angle for additional interest. Should you use the spoon to stir your tea after adding sugar, place it on the saucer. Handling the iced teaspoon when there is no saucer to hold it after stirring is easier to demonstrate than to describe. Keep the long iced teaspoon in your glass, after you stir, with the handle held toward the far side by the index finger and with the remaining three fingers and thumb of the hand, hold the glass while you drink. This is less complicated than it sounds—you quickly absorb this method, and before long your gestures are fluid and you will see that it works beautifully. It is the only possible method when there is no small plate. Practice and those around you will marvel, "Oh, it must be correct because it is handled with such elegance and grace."

This is quite practical since a wet spoon may damage a bare table top or stain fine linens. The etiquette of flatware is that, once used, it should never touch the table again. In a restaurant you may certainly ask for a saucer to place under your glass of iced tea.

Silk Tea Bags

An American, Thomas Sullivan, is credited with creating the tea bag by accident around 1908. To increase product interest, he started sending his retail customers small samples of tea in small hand-sewn silk bags. To his surprise, his customers requested more "bagged" tea, and soon Mr. Sullivan substituted gauze for the silk bag. Today's tea bags are made of filter paper or biodegradeable mesh.

Finessing a Tea Bag

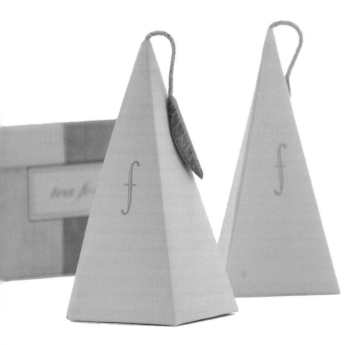

In a restaurant:
When the tea bag is served with a small teapot of water and a cup and saucer: Remove the tea bag from its paper wrapper; place it in the teapot of water, and allow it to steep until it reaches the strength you prefer. After three to five minutes, pour a small amount into your cup to test the strength. Don't pick up the tea bag by the tab on the string and jiggle it up and down to hasten the process. This gives the appearance of impatience.

Do not remove the tea bag from the teapot unless a separate plate is provided for the wet bag. Fold the tea bag wrapper and place it next to the saucer holding the teapot. If you simply can't bear to look at it, fold it and slide it under the saucer holding the teapot.

When ordering tea, you may ask your server if the hot water will be served in a teapot. If the answer is yes, request that the tea bag be placed in the teapot first and the hot water added. You will get a better infusion. (Increase your gratuity for this extra service.)

When a cup of hot water is served with a tea bag placed on the saucer: Remove the tea bag from its paper wrapper and place in the cup of hot water. Allow the tea to steep until it reaches the strength you prefer. Request a saucer to hold the used tea bag. Don't place it on your saucer where it will drain and you will end up with a dripping cup. Never attempt to drain a tea bag by winding the string around a spoon.

Sugar in wrappers and milk in disposable plastic containers: Request a saucer to hold the disposable wrappers and milk containers if one is not provided.

Faux Pas

- Picking up the tea bag by the tab on the string and jiggling it up and down to hasten the steeping process. It doesn't!
- Removing the tea bag from the teapot and placing it on the saucer. This looks messy and you will have a puddle of tea in your saucer that will produce a dripping teacup when you lift it.
- Draining a tea bag by winding the string around a spoon.

T'cha, Paris

8

THE ART OF STEEPING TEA

Tea is nought but this,
First you make the water boil,
Then infuse the tea,
Then you drink it properly,
That is all you need to know.
—Okakura Kakuzo, *The Book of Tea*

Brewing Tea

A few simple steps make the difference between an excellent cup of tea and an ordinary one. The essential ingredients are an electric or stove-top kettle, a teapot (earthenware, porcelain, silver or glass), fresh loose tea leaves, fresh filtered water, and timing.

The Proper Way to Brew a Pot of Black Tea

- Run cold filtered water from the faucet. Fill the tea kettle with sufficient water to warm the teapot and make the tea. (Serious tea drinkers do not heat water in a microwave.)
- When the water is near boiling, pour some into the teapot and swirl it around to warm the teapot. Discard the warming water before adding the tea leaves.
- At this stage, decide if you will place the leaves directly into the teapot (English style) or if you will use a tea infuser or disposable filter. Many teapots come equipped with removable infusion baskets. (Tea balls are less than adequate because they do not allow the wet leaves to fully expand.)
- Measure a rounded teaspoon of tea for each cup of water the teapot holds. Add an extra teaspoon if a stronger tea is preferred.
- When the water comes to a full rolling boil for black tea, take the teapot to the kettle and pour the water onto the tea leaves. Cover the teapot and allow the tea to steep for the desired length of time. A timer is recommended. Remove the tea filter or infuser basket before serving.
- How long to steep? Steeping time depends on several factors: the tea family, the leaf size, and the amount of twist or roll in the leaf. Any black tea should steep at least three minutes; very few require more than five minutes. Darjeeling black teas are the most time-sensitive with 3½ minutes being the usual steeping time.

Most tea merchants include brewing instructions on their labels.

Every tea will taste better if it is "brewed rather than stewed." If you put the leaves directly into the teapot, stir the liquid and strain or decant the steeped tea into another heated teapot. A bitter-tasting "stewy" tea will result from liquor left on the leaves for a long period of time. This may not be offensive if you plan to add milk to your tea.

Water Temperature

Water temperature plays a key role in the production of a good cup of tea. One easily remembered rule is: the lighter the tea, the cooler the water; the darker the tea, the hotter the water. The following water temperatures are recommended.

> White tea and green teas: 165 - 185° F (73-85° C)
> Oolong teas: 185-200° F (85-93° C)
> Black teas, puerh teas, herbals and infusions: boiling

True oolong devotees will want to explore the Gongfu method of infusing and drinking small cups of multiple infusions prepared on a wooden tray and served in small tea cups.

Chinese tea vendor (c. 1890)

Antioxidants, called *flavonoids*, combat free radicals linked to cancer, early aging, and other ills. Drinking tea is an easy and natural source of flavonoids. Like vitamins C and E and beta-carotene, antioxidants inhibit a chemical reaction called *oxidation* that, among other things, can make the body's cells less resistant to cancer-causing agents. In fact, some of the flavonoids in tea are stronger antioxidants than these popular vitamins.

Flavonoids found in black tea are good for the heart and blood vessels in two ways: They prevent the oxidation of LDL cholesterol, which is good because oxidized cholesterol is more damaging to blood vessel walls and more likely to generate plaque. Second, they reduce the clotting tendency of blood.

Green tea contains the powerful catechin EGCG. Research studies on this catechin point to a lower risk of strokes in women, progress in combating Parkinson's disease, and a lower incidence of prostate cancer, among other things. A daily regimen of four to five cups of hot or cold green tea could lead to a healthier lifestyle. Recent tests point to an increased viability of green tea's powerful antioxidant ability if combined with a small amount of citric acid — such as lemon or orange juice.

The other major component of tea is the chemical *theanine,* found in the plant world only in the tea plant. Because it can enter the brain, theanine has psychoactive properties. Theanine has been shown to reduce mental and physical stress, produce feelings of relaxation, and improve cognition and mood when taken in combination with caffeine.

This theanine/caffeine combination may be the key to why tea has always been known for its unique ability to calm our minds while invigorating our spirits. British statesman William Gladstone best described this effect two hundred years ago when he penned these words:

> *"If you are cold, tea will warm you;*
> *If you are too heated, it will cool you;*
> *If you are depressed, it will cheer you;*
> *If you are exhausted, it will calm you."*

Bonthes Thés, Paris

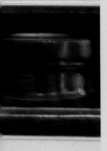

9

___

TEA TYPES

___

Tea gives vigor to the body,
contentment to the mind and
determination of purpose.
—Shen Nung (c. 2737 B.C.E.)

Tea Types

A true *tea* must contain the leaves of the *Camellia sinensis* or *Camellia assamica* plant. There are four primary types, or families, of tea — white, green, oolong, and black. *Camellia* bushes produce leaves and buds that may become any of these family types. The treatment of the leaf after plucking will determine which tea family it joins.

N.º 998

.54 Edwards del. Pub. by T.Curtis, S.ª Geo: Crescent Mar 1 1807 F.Sansom sculp

White Tea

This prized and least-processed tea was first produced from the young unopened tea buds that are gently plucked, withered to remove some moisture, then gently dried. The curled buds have a silvery-white countenance. Originally grown only in the mountains of China's Fujian province, white teas are now also manufactured in Sri Lanka, Kenya and India. The liquor is pale like champagne, and the flavor is soft and smooth with a lingering sweet taste of honey. This expensive all-bud tea is called *Bai Hao Yin Zhen* or *Silver Needle*.

Bai Mudan (or *pai-mu-tan*) is a more abundant and less expensive form of white tea. The top two very young leaves are gently plucked along with the unopened bud. The pickings are slightly withered and immediately dried to keep the tea in its purest form. The un-bruised and lightly-oxidized tea produces a very pale liquor. The growing popularity of white tea and apparent health benefits have led to a proliferation of ready-to-drink white tea beverages and an increase in the number of cosmetic products containing white tea as an ingredient.

White teas are best brewed with 165-175° F water and should be consumed without the addition of milk or sweetener. Multiple infusions are possible when using a gaiwan or *yixing* clay teapot.

Green teas are the oldest of all tea families. Every harvested tea begins as green tea. The freshly plucked two leaves and a bud are either pan-fired in woks, or placed in large mechanical steamers where a 12-minute steam bath kills all the enzymes to prohibit oxidation. The leaves are rolled, either by hand or machine, and dried. Since it is not bruised and oxidized, the dry leaf retains its natural dark olive-green color and its vegetative aroma and taste.

Green tea is becoming known more and more for its health benefits. The buzz word for the past decade has been EGCG, green tea's principle catechin and a strong antioxidant. Researchers worldwide are now looking at EGCG's effect on overall human health, including cancer, Parkinson's disease, and diabetes.

For centuries, China, Japan, and Taiwan were known for green tea production. With the increase in demand, green tea is now produced by every major tea-producing country. Thousands of green teas exist. A few of the best-known include:

Gunpowder: Small, round, yellow-green pellets are hand rolled to resemble their namesake. This common, earthy Chinese tea was a favorite of frontier America and North Africa.

Chunmee: A young, early spring, twisted-leaf Chinese tea that produces a golden-yellow infusion with a pungent aftertaste. Twelve chests of this tea (known by its East Indies Tea Company name *Hyson*) were thrown overboard at the Boston Tea Party on December 16, 1793.

Sencha: This is the most popular Japanese tea. The growing worldwide demand for sencha has prompted Chinese gardens to produce it as well. The long, flat, emerald-green leaves produce a light golden-yellow liquor with a distinct aroma and flavor reminiscent of freshly mown grass. The March to April harvest, now done mechanically, is preferred.

Lung Ching: Originating in the Chinese town of Dragonwell, the best grade of lung ching is made of only the bud and one new leaf. It is not rolled, but left in its natural pointed form. The clean, well-balanced aroma suggests freshly cut grass and toasted chestnuts.

Green teas are best brewed with 175-185° F water and should be consumed without milk.

Oolong Tea

This unique tea is oxidized to a degree between a green tea and a black tea. After a brief withering, the leaves are placed in pans and exposed to high heat, halting the oxidation process. Bags of leaves are then rolled into balls by small machines. The basketball size bags are opened and the curled leaves are separated before being heated over a charcoal fire. Oolongs can be some of the most labor-intensive and expensive teas on the market. In general, the paler the color, the finer the grade. Taiwan and China produce some of the world's most prized handmade oolongs. India, Sri Lanka, and Vietnam have recently entered the market as demand rises. Some of the best-known oolongs include:

Tung Ting: One of Taiwan's premier oolongs comes from high-grown bushes that are shaded from the sun. This tea is lightly oxidized, resulting in a pale subtle liquor with green overtones and a floral aroma.

Ti Kuan Yin: The best known of Chinese oolongs, this aromatic and elegant tea comes from central Fujian province. The slightly twisted leaves unfurl as a mixture of red-brown and dark green colors that release a honey-colored liquor with a delicately sweet floral flavor.

Oolong teas are best brewed with 190-200° F water and should generally be consumed without the addition of milk, lemon, or sweetener. Clay or cast iron pots are preferred for steeping fine oolong teas. Pour hot water over the leaves in the pot and pour off the liquid, thereby giving the leaves a simple quick rinse before infusing. This awakens the leaves and prepares them for the first infusion. The tightly rolled leaves take some time to open. They may be infused up to seven times with each infusion giving off different nuances. You may want to share your response with your fellow drinkers. True oolong devotees will want to explore the Gongfu method of infusing and drinking exceptional teas.

The tea family most consumed by western cultures is black tea. Plucked green leaves are strewn on troughs and allowed to wither for 12 to 24 hours, depending on weather conditions. These limp leaves are in the early stages of oxidation, the principle chemical reaction that determines tea families. After withering, giant rolling machines twist and bruise the leaves, releasing the tea's juices and enzymes. At this stage, the rolled leaves are allowed to oxidize, like compost, for approximately four hours. The oxidation is halted by running the leaves through a drying machine where hot air reduces the moisture. After cooling, the finished tea is cleaned, sorted, and graded before packing. The entire process may take as little as 24 hours in a warm climate. India, Sri Lanka, Kenya, and China are the major exporters of hand-picked black teas.

Black teas may be offered as single-estate, blended, or flavored teas. A few of the most popular black teas appearing on tea menus include:

Assam: A robust, malty tea from the northeast Indian state of Assam where over 800 tea gardens are cultivated. It is often manufactured to be consumed with milk and can be found in many breakfast blends, Irish blends, and inexpensive tea bags.

Darjeeling: A delicate, slightly-green, black tea from the Himalayan foothills of India. Eighty-six tea gardens in Darjeeling produce only 4% of the world's teas. These exceptional, high-grown teas are among the most expensive and prized. The four yearly pickings are First Flush, Second Flush, Rainy Teas, and Autumnal Flush. Darjeelings are perfect for accompanying afternoon tea foods. They may be consumed with or without milk.

Earl Grey: The world's most popular flavored tea is a simple blend of any black tea scented with oil of bergamot, derived from a small citrus fruit found in the Mediterranean region. Most tea purveyors would suggest drinking it plain or with the addition of a bit of sugar.

Keemun: This classic black tea comes from the Anhui province of China. Its earthy overtones and satisfying flavor combine to make a brew that has been a favorite for over a century. It makes a delicious morning brew or an accompaniment for afternoon tea.

Lapsang Souchong: This hearty and distinctively flavored tea from Taiwan or China is smoked over a bed of smoldering pine needles. Tea drinkers either love it or hate it. It was one of Winston Churchill's favorites. It is the perfect accompaniment for savory dishes on a cold day.

Orange Pekoe: Many tea blenders offer a tea called "Orange Pekoe." It is not a blend and has nothing to do with oranges. Orange Pekoe, or OP, is a grade of tea, usually from either India or Sri Lanka. Some tea merchants use the term to name a fine quality black tea, good for all-day consumption either with or without milk.

Black teas should be made with water that is close to boiling.

Herbals and Infusions

Rooibos or *Red Bush tea:* This caffeine-free herbal infusion is made from the bark of a bush that is grown in the southern tip of Africa. It is full-bodied and high in Vitamin C. American consumers tend to prefer it blended with spices or flavorings.

Tisanes: This French word is used to describe any blend of herbs, flowers, fruit, roots, berries, bark, or the leaves of any plant other than *Camellia sinensis*. Tisanes do not contain caffeine. Peppermint, chamomile, and ginger are common herbal tisanes. Strawberries, apples, blueberries, and other dried fruits make delicious fruit infusions especially enjoyed by children.

Harrods Food Hall, London

Visitors to London, mesmerized by the incredibly creative food halls of Harrods or Fortnum & Mason, are inclined to purchase great quantities of souvenir tins containing English tea. Once home, these decorative tins sometimes sit in the pantry for years. Should these teas be consumed after sitting that long? No. The brewed tea won't hurt you but it will lose much of its flavor after a year of neglect. Discard the tea leaves and keep the souvenir tin as a wonderful memory, or refill it with fresh tea.

Because humidity is the number one enemy of tea, it needs to be kept dry. Use tins, containers with lids, or a light-proof glass bottle with a tight cover. Tea easily picks up odors. Store unflavored teas away from flavored teas, spices, or aromatic produce.

Buy tea in small amounts and replenish it often. If your tea is more than one year old, sprinkle the leaves around your garden flowers and buy fresh stock. Flavored teas and herbals are best enjoyed within nine months of the purchase date.

Keep these simple rules in mind:
- Store tea in a cool, dark place away from heat and sunlight.
- Store tea in small amounts.
- Store tea away from odors.
- Green tea stored in a refrigerator needs to be sealed in an airtight plastic bag and kept in a tea can.
- If your tea is more than one year old, toss it and buy fresh tea.

The Hazelmere Cafe, Grange-over-Sands, England

10

RECIPES

*Men's phobia about tea rooms makes them
miss a lot of good eating.*
—Duncan Hines (1880-1959)

Apricot, Globe Grape, and Blue Cheese Tea Sandwiches

Spread

¾ cup garlic and herb spreadable cream cheese

¼ cup crumbled blue cheese

¼ cup dried apricots, chopped

24 large red globe grapes

24 pieces of cocktail party rye bread

Fresh chives or scallions, chopped

Mix together cream cheese, blue cheese, and apricots.

Cut grapes in half and remove any seed particles.

Spread cheese mixture on each slice of bread. Cut in half to make a triangle.

Place a grape half, sliced side down, on top of each triangle. Garnish with chives.

Can be prepared up to 6 hours ahead when covered with a lightly dampened tea towel, and placed in an airtight plastic container.

Makes 48 tea sandwiches.

Benedictine Tea Sandwiches

Spread

2 medium cucumbers, peeled and seeded

12 ounces cream cheese, softened to room temperature

1 small onion, grated

Salt to taste

Mayonnaise

1 loaf wheat bread, crust removed and cut into diamond shapes

Grate cucumbers and blot with a paper towel to remove excess moisture.

Combine grated cucumbers with cream cheese.

Blend in onion and salt to taste.

Stir in a little mayonnaise just to make the mixture spreadable.

Spread mixture evenly over pieces of bread.

Garnish with a thin slice of cucumber and parsley.

Makes about 45 small open-faced sandwiches.

Stuffed Tea Muffins

Muffins
¾ cup milk
⅓ cup melted butter
¼ cup frozen orange juice concentrate, thawed
2 teaspoons grated orange peel
1 egg, slightly beaten
2¼ cups all-purpose flour
½ cup sugar
3 teaspoons baking powder
¼ teaspoon salt
¼ cup sugar
1¼ teaspoons grated orange peel

Heat oven to 400° F. Grease bottoms of 36 mini-muffin cups.
In a large bowl, whisk milk, butter, juice concentrate, 2 teaspoons orange peel, and egg.
Stir together flour, ½ cup sugar, baking powder, and salt.
Add to liquid mixture and stir only until moistened. Spoon into muffin cups.
Combine ¼ cup sugar and orange peel. Sprinkle over batter in cups.
Bake 10-15 minutes or until light golden brown.
Let stand 5 minutes, then remove from pan and cool completely.

Spread
2 cups baked ham, finely-ground
¼ cup orange marmalade
1 teaspoon stone ground mustard

Mix ham, orange marmalade and ground mustard to make a chunky spread. Make a
vertical cut halfway through muffin. Stuff with ham mixture. Garnish with fresh parsley.

Chicken and Olive Tea Sandwich

9 ounces cooked chicken breasts, diced
½ cup green pimento-stuffed olives, drained and thinly sliced
⅓ cup diced pimentos, drained
4 medium green onions, finely chopped
¼ cup sour cream
1 loaf good sandwich bread, cut into forty 2-inch rounds

Combine chicken, olives, pimentos, and green onions in medium mixing bowl.
Moisten with sour cream until mixture is spreadable.
Using a spreading knife, cover each bread round with 1 tablespoon chicken mixture.
Garnish with 2 to 3 olive slices.
Can be prepared up to 6 hours ahead when covered with a lightly dampened
tea towel and placed in an airtight plastic container.
Makes 40 sandwiches.

Classic Scones

2 cups all-purpose flour
2 teaspoons baking powder
½ teaspoon salt
¼ teaspoon baking soda
6 tablespoons unsalted cold butter
½ cup currants
½ cup buttermilk
1 egg
1 tablespoon cream
1 tablespoon sugar

Preheat the oven to 400° F. Lightly grease a large baking sheet.
Combine flour, baking powder, salt, and soda.
With a pastry blender, cut in butter, mixing it until the mixture
resembles coarse crumbs. Mix in currants.

Whisk buttermilk and egg together, then add to flour mixture.
Stir together until a soft ball of dough forms.
Turn onto a lightly floured surface and knead gently, turning five or six times.

Roll out dough with a floured rolling pin to about ½-inch thickness.
Using a cookie cutter, cut scones out and place on the baking sheet.
Brush tops lightly with cream and sprinkle with sugar.
Bake 10 to 12 minutes or until light brown.
Serve warm with lemon curd, clotted cream, or preserves.
Makes one dozen scones.

Lemon Curd

3 eggs
½ cup fresh lemon juice
1 cup sugar
½ cup unsalted butter, melted

In the top part of a double boiler, beat eggs until frothy.
Stir in lemon juice, sugar, and melted butter.
Place over simmering water.
Stir constantly for 20 minutes. The mixture should become slightly thickened.
Remove from heat and spoon into a pint-sized container.
Cool to room temperature, cover and refrigerate before serving.
Keeps well for two weeks.

Brownie Tea Cakes

¾ cup butter
2 squares semi-sweet chocolate
1 square unsweetened chocolate
1¾ cups sugar
4 eggs
1 teaspoon vanilla extract
1 cup all-purpose flour
2 tablespoons cocoa
⅛ teaspoon salt
1 cup walnuts, toasted and chopped
Powdered sugar

Preheat oven to 350° F. Melt butter and chocolate over low heat.
Remove from heat and stir in sugar.
Add eggs, one at a time, stirring well with each addition.
Add vanilla.
Combine flour, cocoa, and salt. Add this to the chocolate mixture.
Stir with a wire whisk until smooth. Stir in chopped walnuts.

Spoon batter into paper-lined mini-muffin tins, filling ¾ full.
Bake 12 to 15 minutes. Cool and dust with powdered sugar.
Makes 32 brownie cakes.

Shortbread Hearts

2 cups unsalted butter
1 cup granulated sugar
1 teaspoon almond extract
Dash of salt
4 cups all-purpose flour
1 cup finely chopped almonds
1 cup powdered sugar

Preheat oven to 325° F.
In a large bowl, beat granulated sugar and butter until fluffy.
Add almond extract and a dash of salt. Beat well.
Add flour and almonds. Mix well.
Roll out on a floured board to ¼-inch thickness.
Cut with a heart-shaped cookie cutter.

Place the cookies on an ungreased cookie sheet. Bake for 15-20 minutes.
Cookies should not brown. Cool on a wire rack.

Glaze
Mix together 1 cup powdered sugar and just enough warm water
to make a spreadable icing.
Add a touch of red food coloring to give the mixture a pink tint.
Spread the icing in a heart pattern on each cookie.

Lemon Bars

1½ cups unbleached all-purpose flour
1 teaspoon baking powder
½ teaspoon salt
One 15-ounce can sweetened condensed milk
¼ teaspoon lemon oil
½ cup lemon juice
5⅓ ounces butter
1 cup dark brown sugar, firmly packed
1 cup old-fashioned or quick-cooking oats

Preheat oven to 325° F. Sift together flour, baking powder, and salt. Set aside.

Combine condensed milk, lemon oil, and juice in a medium-sized mixing bowl.
Stir with a wire whisk until smooth and thick. Set aside.

In a large bowl, cream the butter and brown sugar.
Add sifted ingredients, then oats. Mixture will be crumbly.
Pat 2 cups of crumbs into bottom of a greased 9x13-inch pan.
Spread condensed milk mixture atop crumb layer.
Sprinkle remaining crumb mixture over layer, smoothing gently.

Bake for 30-35 minutes, or until bars are brown around the edges.
Remove from oven and cool completely.
Cut into small squares and refrigerate.
Bring to room temperature before serving.
Makes 30 bars.

Victorian Tea Cake

Cake
¾ cup butter, softened
¾ cup sugar
3 eggs, beaten
1½ cups self-rising flour
4 teaspoons boiling water

Preheat oven to 325° F. Grease two 8-inch round cake pans and line with wax paper.
In a large bowl, beat together butter and sugar until light and fluffy.
Add eggs one at a time. Fold in flour.
Add boiling water to make a soft batter.
Divide batter evenly and pour into prepared pans.
Bake 25-30 minutes or until cakes are lightly browned. Cool in pans for 5 minutes.
Remove cakes from pans. Remove wax paper. Transfer to wire rack to cool competely.

Raspberry Curd Filling
3 eggs, beaten
½ cup unsalted butter, melted and cooled
1 cup sugar
½ cup raspberry puree (fresh or frozen raspberries may be used)

In a double boiler, beat eggs until frothy. Stir in butter, sugar and raspberry puree.
Place over simmering water and stir constantly for 20 minutes until slightly thickened.
Remove from heat. Spoon into container. Cool to room temperature. Refrigerate.

Frosting
1 cup powdered sugar, sifted
2 teaspoons lemon juice

Mix together powdered sugar and lemon juice. Add small amount of water, if needed, to make a good consistency for drizzling over cake. Place one cake on a cake plate. Spread top with Raspberry Curd. Top with second cake. Drizzle frosting in a crisscross pattern.

117

INDEX

INDEX